THE BELIEVER'S AUTHORITY

What You Didn't Learn in Church

by
Andrew Wommack

Harrison House
Tulsa, Oklahoma

Unless otherwise indicated, all Scripture quotations are taken from the *King James Version* of the Bible.

The author has emphasized some words in Scripture quotations in italicized type.

21 20 19 23 22 21 20 19

The Believer's Authority
What You Didn't Learn in Church
ISBN 13: 978-1-57794-936-7
ISBN 10: 1-57794-936-6

P.O. Box 3333
Colorado Springs, CO 80934-3333
www.awmi.net

Published by Harrison House Publishers
Tulsa, Oklahoma 74145
www.harrisonhouse.com

Contents

Introduction

Most people have a humanistic view of how life works. Even though Christians don't like this terminology, many of them function day by day with this same mentality. By only looking on the surface level, they don't recognize the spirit realm behind it all.

Humanists don't acknowledge God. As a whole, they're either agnostic or atheist—believing that everything in life has a natural, physical cause. It's sad to say, but many Christians have this same attitude. They don't realize the spiritual dynamics behind what's happening in the physical realm.

We are in a spiritual battle! Every single day, there is a battle raging in the spirit realm for the heart of each individual person, society, and the world as a whole. God is trying to draw us toward Himself and righteousness. He's trying to influence us to live consistently with Him so that His blessings can manifest in our lives. At the same time, Satan is trying to steal our hearts away from God. In an all-out battle against the Lord and His kingdom, the enemy is pouring all the trash and corruption he can into our lives.

Most of us—even Christians—don't recognize the intense battle being waged all around us each and every day. We don't know the spiritual significance of our choices, words, and actions. We're functionally ignorant of how these things determine whether we're yielded to God and releasing His power and blessing into our lives, or yielded to Satan and releasing sin and death into our lives. (Rom. 6:16.)

The devil can't control you outside of your will. However, your lack of awareness and understanding of the battle only works to his advantage. If you choose to believe God's Word and learn to recognize what's happening in the spirit realm, you can begin taking the proper action to improve your situation. You can cooperate with God to manifest His power and blessings.

> Submit yourselves therefore to God. Resist the devil, and he will flee from you.
>
> JAMES 4:7

You *can* resist the devil, and he *will* flee from you. Your passivity and lack of resistance doesn't mean that the battle isn't raging. It just simply means that you aren't winning. Satan is beating you in this area.

The revelation of God's Word contained in this book has the potential of transforming your life. As you begin to understand and exercise your authority as a believer in the Lord Jesus Christ, Satan will flee and God's power and blessings will manifest in your life greater than ever before.

CHAPTER 1

We're in a Spiritual Battle

> Finally, my brethren, be strong in the Lord, and in the power of his might. Put on the whole armour of God, that ye may be able to stand against the wiles of the devil. For we wrestle not against flesh and blood, but against principalities, against powers, against the rulers of the darkness of this world, against spiritual wickedness in high places.
>
> EPHESIANS 6:10–12

God's Word reveals that we are not wrestling against flesh and blood, but demonic powers. Our fight isn't against people, but the spiritual forces influencing them. However, most of us simply don't recognize the role that the spirit realm plays in what occurs in our daily life. We think it's just human—natural—but the devil is busy influencing people every day.

It's useless to debate whether or not an individual is possessed, oppressed, or just depressed. When the New Testament calls someone *demon-possessed,* the Greek word there literally means "demonized."[1] They are under the influence—and therefore, control—of the devil.[2] This issue people make about whether someone is possessed, oppressed, or just depressed isn't in the Scriptures. The truth is that people all around the world today are being influenced, controlled, and used—to whatever degree—by the devil.

Proper Perspective

Many westerners honestly believe that all the demons are over in some third-world country. But anyone who is spiritually perceptive knows that there is an abundance of demonic activity anywhere you go in the world, including the West. We just tend to look at things as being normal and natural for this day and age. We miss the fact that the origin of many things that happen in our day—things that tick us off and come against us—is spiritual. We fail to recognize the spiritual influence behind it.

If you were to adopt the biblical mindset, it would make a huge difference in the way you respond. You'd recognize that it's not that person who sits next to you at work, it's not your neighbor, your spouse, or your circumstances that are really what's coming against you. They can be influenced, inspired, and used of Satan, but they themselves aren't really the source. When you genuinely understand that this isn't a physical battle, it changes the way you respond.

I get a lot of hate mail and criticism because of the things I say. There was a time when I took these things personally and thought, *Why is this individual so upset with me?* I just looked at their criticisms and always tried to deal with them on the human level. Since then, I've come to recognize that Satan is the one who's trying to get my attention off of what God has told me to do. I recognize that the enemy is using some person to come against me. He's trying to gain an inroad into my life so he can steal God's Word from me. (Mark 4:16–17.) But because I look beyond the individual and don't take their comments personally, I'm able to put things into proper perspective and deal with it differently.

I've actually had some good friends come against me. Even though they did some pretty mean things, I've been able to look past that and forgive them. I recognized that they had a sensitivity in some area that Satan took advantage of and used them against me. I haven't been angry or bitter toward them because I understood what the devil was trying to do. Since then, they've turned around and realized what happened. We've been able to completely reestablish our friendship because I recognized that it wasn't those people, but Satan trying to get at me.

Satan Uses People

Jesus exemplified this same perspective. He recognized when the devil was trying to get to Him through a person.

After Peter—under the influence of God—confessed Jesus as "the Christ, the Son of the living God" (Matt. 16:16), the Lord started explaining to His disciples about His soon coming crucifixion, death, and resurrection. Immediately, Peter began to rebuke Him, saying:

> Be it far from thee, Lord: this shall not be unto thee.
>
> MATTHEW 16:22

Apparently, Peter had missed Jesus' statement that He would rise again on the third day. Peter didn't even want to consider the thought of his beloved Lord being taken and killed. This was the same man who just moments before had been inspired and controlled by the Holy Spirit. Yet now Jesus...

> Turned, and said unto Peter, Get thee behind me, Satan: thou art an offence unto me: for thou savourest not the things that be of God, but those that be of men.
>
> MATTHEW 16:23

The Lord recognized that Satan was speaking through Peter. This wasn't something coming from God. Jesus knew it was inconsistent with what the Father had clearly revealed to Him of His will. So even though Peter had previously spoken forth a glorious revelation by the Holy Spirit, Christ knew that the inspiration for this rebuke was from hell.

There are times when the devil speaks to you through people. He'll use people to get at you. Of course, they may be unaware of the fact that they're being used of Satan. Peter was probably shocked, hurt, and offended when Jesus turned around and said, "Get behind me, Satan!" However, there are times when you need to rebuke the devil that way too.

Whose Voice Is It?

Now don't misunderstand me and go around blasting people. I'm not saying you should rebuke everyone who disagrees with you, declaring, "You're of the devil. Satan is using you in my life." That's not what I'm trying to get across. You just need to recognize that Satan—as well as God—can speak through and use the people in your life. Like Jesus, you need to discern whose voice is coming through.

More than thirty years ago, my mother wanted to take my wife, my oldest son (who was one at the time), and me to the Smoky Mountains. This was back during our "poverty days." Jamie and I were struggling financially and didn't have any money, but since Mother offered to pay for everything on the trip, we decided to go ahead and go.

At that time, my mother had just started believing God for healing. Since she hadn't seen the manifestation yet in the specific areas she'd been believing for, basically she had suffered a defeat.

Due to this, Mother was on the bubble about whether this "healing stuff" really worked or not. Since then, she's turned around and received great healing, but this was way back in the beginning of our ministry when Mother still thought I was somewhere out on the lunatic fringe.

Anyway, as we began our trip, Mother was nursing a little bit of a cold. She started saying negative things about my son like, "Keep him away from me or he'll catch this cold."

I'd answer, "No, Mother. He's not going to catch this cold."

Then she'd complain about the money, saying, "I really shouldn't be taking this trip. I don't have the money to do it."

So I just told her, "Hey, Mother. We have zippo, zilch, nada. If you don't have the money to take this trip, we need to go home now because I can't help you."

She'd respond, "Oh no! I've got plenty of money." Mother was just in a negative mindset, which made it a bad situation.

During the hot summer day, my son sat right in front of the air conditioner. Since I understood that we can have what we say (Mark 11:23), it really bothered me when she said things like, "Don't put him there. He'll catch a cold!"

I'd have to counter that with, "No, he's not going to catch a cold."

"Shut Up!"

All this griping and complaining was really out of character for my mother. She is a super lady and is usually very positive, but she was just stuck in this negative mindset. She talked doubt and unbelief all day long. It was a constant battle back and forth to counter what was being said. Since this was my mother, I tried to be as polite and kind as I possibly could.

The very first night of the trip, we all stayed in a hotel room together. Our son was sleeping in a little crib. Around eleven o'clock, he woke up with this croup in his throat that you could have heard in the next room. It was loud and he could hardly breathe, so I got up, prayed in tongues, rebuked the croup, and released my faith. He went back to sleep and everything was fine.

Thirty minutes later, the same thing happened. I got up, prayed over him, and he went back to sleep. Every thirty minutes, I was up and down like a yo-yo, praying over our son and trying to get him back to sleep. Finally, about three in the morning on one of my trips back to bed, my mother said, "Admit it, Andy. He's sick!"

I got right down there, stuck my finger in her face, and said, "Satan, in the name of Jesus, I command you to shut up! I will not receive any of your criticism or any of your curses. My son is blessed and not cursed!" Then I started speaking the Word. Mother never said another word, and our son never got up again that night. He was just fine, but Mother didn't say anything for two whole days—and we were together all the time in a car on vacation.

Finally, when she did speak, she cried, "Well, I'm sorry you think I'm the devil" and started into this self-pity party.

I said, "Mother, you know enough to know better. I've told you the Word of God. You knew that stuff you were saying was exactly opposite the Word. You'd just given yourself over to Satan. I'm not mad at you. I was just standing against the devil. He was trying to steal my faith for healing."

To this day, Mother continues to be one of my very best friends. She's over ninety five years old and enjoys the blessing of good health. My approach that night was pretty strong, but I knew Satan was behind this attack trying to steal my faith.

You can certainly take a stand against what people say with more tact than I displayed back then. I was young in the Lord and that's just the way I responded, but the principle applies regardless of how you administer it.

Stretched to the Max

We are in a spiritual battle! Unfortunately, most of the time people don't recognize it. They're just looking at things from a natural, human perspective. They factor God, the devil, and the whole supernatural realm right out of the equation. The average person doesn't realize the spiritual dynamics taking place. God doesn't send bad things our way. It's not just happenstance or fate. There's a real enemy out there that we must learn to deal with.

The first time I tried to produce a book was about twenty years ago. It was my *Life for Today—Gospels Edition* study Bible and commentary, which is almost six hundred pages long. This was going to be a major expense. At that time, my ministry income was so low that to come up with $50,000 to print a book was two or three months' worth of income for me. This project was really stretching me to the max!

A number of different publishers came and offered to help us with the project. One offered to reduce our cost to $27,000 if we would pay right away. They said, "We're in a bind and need the money. If you pay right away, we'll give you this discount." So I went to my partners, raised the money—more than a month's worth of income at the time—and gave it to them. This was a major deal for us.

Within a month, I learned that the salesman had run off with our money. In fact, he'd burned several other well-known preachers at the same time!

I remember when I heard this news. My employee said, "This salesman just took our $27,000. We're going to have to come up with an additional $45,000 just in the next week or so to be able to make this project work. All together, we're looking at about $70,000."

Sevenfold

My first reaction was shock. *Is this really true?* Then came a fleshly twinge of wanting to beat up this salesman. But I recognized who the real culprit was. Satan had come against me and was trying to steal from me.

Immediately, Proverbs 6:31 came to mind.

> But if [a thief] be found, he shall restore sevenfold; he shall give all the substance of his house.

I recognized that this wasn't just a person trying to steal from me. Obviously, there were demonic entities working behind the scenes. So within seconds of getting this news, I realized, *This is the devil stealing from me, and I've caught him. Therefore, according to the Word of God, I demand it back seven times!* Immediately, I took a piece of paper and figured out seven times $70,000. Instead of being angry, depressed, and hurt, I started dancing and praising God, saying, "Hallelujah, this is awesome. I'm getting $490,000 back *this* year!" As I continued praising God, that situation never did get me down or discouraged.

When that year was over, we had increased nearly to the penny $490,000—exactly seven times the amount of money that was taken from us. That was back during a period of time when our entire income was only about $500,000 a year. We nearly doubled our income that year!

What could have been a tragic scenario turned into a positive situation because I recognized that I'm not fighting flesh and blood. I'm fighting a spiritual battle, with spiritual weapons, against spiritual enemies. I realized that Satan was trying to come against me, and then acted on the Word.

Who's Influencing Whom?

I've actually loaned people money before who have never paid me back. They said they would, but for whatever reason, they didn't. Instead of taking an offense and getting mad at the person, I recognize that this is Satan. Of course, the person cooperated in some measure and allowed him to do it, but I recognize that the devil was trying to get me into unforgiveness. So I just forgive them. My attitude is, "Hey, just take it as a gift. I'm not going to sit here and harbor any animosity over this. It's not worth it."

You might think, *Man, I'd never do something like that.* But I recognize that there is a spiritual battle raging—and nobody is going to rent space in my mind! Nobody is going to occupy my heart except God. I refuse to harbor unforgiveness toward anyone. I will not allow bitterness even a toehold in my life. I'm aware that Satan uses such things as an inroad against me.

Like it or not, there's a spiritual battle raging right now for your heart and mind. As you think in your heart is the way that you'll be. (Prov. 23:7.) Your thoughts become what you say and do, with your actions being the greatest expression of your authority. Therefore, you'll be influenced, dominated, and ruled by whomever you yield yourself to—God or Satan.

CHAPTER 2

Whom He May Devour

When you yield yourself to sin, you're serving Satan, who is the author of that sin. But when you yield yourself to obedience, you serve God, who is the author of that righteousness.

> Know ye not, that to whom ye yield yourselves servants to obey, his servants ye are to whom ye obey; whether of sin unto death, or of obedience unto righteousness?
>
> ROMANS 6:16

In this spiritual battle, your actions are very important.

Most people recognize that actions are important in the physical realm. You know that there are consequences for what you do. If you're speeding while driving, you could get a ticket or cause a wreck. The ticket could cost money and put points on your license. The wreck could damage cars or even cost someone their life. When we talk negatively about someone, we can hurt their feelings or even loose demonic powers against them.

There's much more to life than just this physical, natural, surface level. Spiritual dynamics are constantly taking place. Whether or not the person you're speaking evil about ever knows it, you'll be affected. Venting anger, frustration, resentment, or unforgiveness affects you whether it affects anyone else or not. I've actually ridden with people who are very vocal in traffic when someone cuts them off. They've told me, "That person doesn't know what I said. They didn't hear me." It doesn't matter whether they ever hear you or not. If you get angry and bitter, you've just yielded yourself to Satan. Whether you recognize it or not, the devil is the one who influences us to respond in the wrong way.

The Wrath of Man

James 1:20 says, "The wrath of man worketh not the righteousness of God." In other words, giving place to anger and bitterness doesn't accomplish the righteousness of God. You aren't going to accomplish God's purposes by getting in the flesh, giving in to anger, and losing your temper. That's not the way God's kingdom works. So whether anyone else ever hears you or not—what you say is having an effect on you.

A fellow I led to the Lord some time ago was genuinely converted and had come quite a ways in his discipleship. He upholstered cars and was trying to restore a certain old one. One day, I went over to his house and knocked on the door but there was no answer. I knew he was home, so I walked around to the backyard. As I came around the corner of his house, I heard this awful profanity, screaming, and yelling. This brother had a fence post and was beating the fire out of that car!

He was cussing this car up and down as I—his pastor—came around the corner. When he saw me, he stopped for a moment (conviction, I presume) and said, "Well, it's just a car. It's doesn't matter what I say to it. I didn't hurt anybody." I had to explain to him that it didn't matter what it was. When you give place to anger and vent like that, Satan jumps on it like a chicken on a June bug. The enemy will take full advantage of an open door like that to come and steal, kill, and destroy. (John 10:10.)

> Where envying and strife is, there is confusion and *every* evil work.
>
> JAMES 3:16

Notice how this didn't say, "some" evil works. It didn't say envying and strife "could" allow the devil to come against "certain types of people." No, when you get into envy and strife, you're flinging the door wide open and saying, "Come on in Satan and do your worst in my life." You're drawing a great big target on your back and saying, "Shoot your best shot!" When you give in to envy and strife, you make yourself a target for the devil.

Are You Spiritually Stinky?

> We are unto God a sweet savour [smell] of Christ, in them that are saved, and in them that perish.
>
> 2 CORINTHIANS 2:15

What is your spiritual scent? Are you giving off the sweet aroma of Christ, or are you spiritually stinky? Just like flies and rats, demons are attracted to open wounds and garbage in your life. Your rotten attitude—getting mad in traffic, being bitter over whatever, and criticizing everything and everyone—is putting out an aroma that's drawing every demon in the county to your house. And you wonder, *Why am I having these problems? Why does nothing go right for me?* That's just ignorance gone to seed. You need to recognize that we're in a spiritual battle. Your thoughts, attitudes, words, and actions are either releasing the power of God in your life, or they're releasing the power of the devil.

You might think, *Fate is against me. I have bad luck.* You may even put it off on the Lord, saying, "God, why have You allowed these things to happen to me?" It's not like that at all. God is good and He's doing everything He can to save, bless, heal, and prosper you. However, we do have an enemy who is going around looking for anyone he may destroy.

> Be sober, be vigilant; because your adversary the devil, as a roaring lion, walketh about, seeking whom he may devour.
>
> 1 PETER 5:8

Notice that it's "whom he *may* devour." Satan cannot devour (or destroy[1]) you without your cooperation. One way he gains that cooperation is through ignorance. You may think that it doesn't matter if you get mad at the car you're working on, or the driver who just cut you off in traffic. You might think that nobody's harmed when you gossip about someone who isn't there, saying, "They won't hear this." But the truth is, once you start venting these things, Satan takes advantage of it.

For some reason or another, we feel like politicians are just fair game. We think we're free to say anything we want about them because the freedom of speech our country enjoys encourages us to voice our disagreement. However, there is a right and wrong way to do it. I've heard Christians rail on a presidential candidate or some other public officer in ways that aren't healthy. You can disagree without putting a person to shame with the words you say. It doesn't matter whether they ever hear you or not. You could be opening up a door to the devil through your words. (Rom. 6:16.)

Spiritual Dynamics

You need to set a watch before your mouth (Ps. 141:3) and take every thought captive to the obedience of Christ. (2 Cor. 10:5.) You need to control your actions (Gal. 5:22–24) and recognize that the demonic realm is trying to take a shot at you every day of your life. If you allow a door to be opened to them, they'll come in for no other purpose than to steal, kill, and destroy. (John 10:10.) Remember, Satan is looking for whom he may devour.

You need to learn to recognize the spiritual dynamics happening in your life. God wants you to yield to Him so that His power and blessings can be released in you. Satan wants you to yield to him so that destruction and death can be released in you. In order to gain an inroad, the enemy is constantly trying to snare you with bitterness, unforgiveness, and ungodliness of all kinds. Therefore, no matter what you do, you're either obeying God or obeying Satan. You're either submitting to God and His influence or to Satan and his influence. Every time you act, you are releasing spiritual power—either God's or the devil's—into your life. Since most people are ignorant of this truth, they allow all kinds of things in their life. Yet, if they were to recognize the results they're going to reap, they would never allow these things.

At one time the wife of one of our Bible college students was suffering from severe depression. When I began to tell her how she could be delivered from this, she explained that she had battled depression since she was a little girl. She'd go through a period of one or two months each year where she would be severely depressed and have to treat it with medication.

When I told her, "You don't want to live that way anymore; you need to get over this," she answered, "This is just the way that I am. It's not hurting anything. I get over it. Everything's okay in a month or so." She had totally accepted and embraced this depression, thinking it was only a passing thing that had no lasting impact. But every time we submit to doing things Satan's way, we are having spiritual relations with him, which conceives evil. It isn't just benign.

Sin's Conception

> Every man is tempted, when he is drawn away of his own lust, and enticed. Then when lust hath conceived, it bringeth forth sin: and sin, when it is finished, bringeth forth death.
>
> JAMES 1:14,15

Sin is conceived in your emotions. Every time you have a negative emotion—whether it be sadness, anger, fear, strife, or one of many others—you conceive something. Many people are conceiving things that they don't want to birth. They don't want depression, strife, suicide, or their marriage to fall apart. Yet they allow these negative emotions to flow through them without recognizing that we're in a spiritual battle. When you give in to your flesh and start saying and doing these things, you are releasing spiritual forces. There is a battle raging and the enemy is looking for an opportunity to come against you.

The devil's will is to devour everyone he can. (1 Pet. 5:8.) He desires to steal, kill, and destroy every person everywhere. (John 10:10.) If Satan got what he wanted, then the whole earth would be devastated, and there would be no good anywhere.

However, God has a will too. Jesus said:

> I am come that they might have life, and that they might have it more abundantly.
>
> JOHN 10:10

Jesus is trying to release life into you. Satan is trying to steal, kill, and destroy anything good that you have. Both are willing and able to move and manifest those things in your life, but the determining factor is you. You need to recognize this battle that's raging and the fact that everything you say and do is either empowering God or the devil. The Lord wants to release His life into you. Satan wants to steal that life and kill and destroy you. It's not fate or luck. Your thoughts, choices, and actions make a huge difference in your life.

"Get Out of My Life!"

I visited a church once that had previously believed God could heal, but that it wasn't His will to heal every single time. What I didn't know was that less than six months before I came, they had changed their mind to come into agreement with the Word, saying, "It's God's will for every person to be well. He heals all the time." This was a brand-new step of faith for them. The congregation was beginning to hear the Word and starting to believe God for specific manifestations of healing.

Two days before I arrived, that church had a funeral for a seventeen-year-old boy who had died after being in a coma for six weeks. The entire church had fasted and prayed, trying to implement the truths from God's Word that they were being taught. Although they knew it was God's will to heal this boy, he died anyway. The outcome caused a tremendous amount of conflict, turmoil, and questions in that church.

After the morning meetings, I went out to eat with the parents of the boy every day for three days trying to figure out exactly what had transpired. Since everyone had given it their best shot—doing everything they knew to do—many people in the church were beginning to back off the Word, saying, "Maybe it's not God's will to heal every time." When I told them that wasn't true—that God had already provided healing and it's His will to heal every single time—they responded, "Well then, what's the problem?"

As I talked with the boy's parents those three days, I discovered that they had been in so much strife that they were about to get a divorce. They'd already made the plans and had talked about it with the children. So there was much strife, hurt, and negative emotion in that home.

On the morning of the tragedy, the mother had an argument with this boy and told him, "I hate you. Get out of my house and never come back again!" She probably didn't mean what she said. She was just saying it out of the heat of emotion. I know that kids can sometimes get on your nerves. I've raised some myself. Raising kids is harder than raising the dead—and I've had to do both in my family! I'm not trying to condemn this lady, but before this boy left, she said, "Get out of my life and never come back again."

Every Evil Work

Because the boy had been hurt by his mom, he violated school policy that day, left the school grounds, and went over to another kid's house to eat lunch. While there, they got out a gun, were playing with it, and the boy accidentally shot himself in the head. That's the reason he had been in a coma for six weeks.

The parents just didn't understand how this could have happened. The Word reveals that "Where envying and strife is, there is confusion and *every* evil work" (James 3:16).

Many people say, "I agree that strife isn't the best. Nobody likes it, but it's just a normal part of life. Families fight, and then they get over it." Without realizing that we're in a spiritual battle, they just tolerate different levels of strife in their life. The Word says that envying and strife bring confusion.

> God is not the author of confusion, but of peace.
>
> 1 Corinthians 14:33

If God isn't the author of confusion, guess who is? That's right—Satan. The devil is the one who—wherever envying and strife are—brings confusion and every evil work.

When you fling a door open like that to the devil, don't be surprised if you see different forms of sickness, tragedy, poverty, and death manifest. Satan jumps on opportunities like that and uses them as inroads into your life. As a roaring lion, he's constantly seeking whom he may devour.

CHAPTER 3

Satan's Inroads

Since we're in a spiritual battle, you can't afford to indulge the "luxury" of strife. If you think that a certain amount of strife is just normal—the way we're supposed to live—you're wrong. God is a God of peace (Rom. 15:33; 16:20), and we were created in His image. (Gen. 1:27.) The fruit of His Spirit working in our life is peace. (Gal. 5:22.) Therefore, our life should be full of peace, not strife. I'm not saying that we will ever live totally free from all strife from every source, but you should never just accept it, indulge it, or promote it. You ought to actively stand against and fight it, recognizing that every time you get into strife a door is opened for anything the enemy wants to do in your life. Satan has access to you when you're in strife.

I remember being drafted as a soldier in the army. During basic training, there were many situations where explosions were going off around me all the time. We'd go out on maneuvers, pass through low-crawl pits (with machine guns firing overhead), learn how to use grenades, practice firing our weapons, and many other things. Over a period of six months' time in training, I became accustomed to all the noise. It didn't bother me because I knew that we were still in our own country, it was training, and nobody was trying to kill me.

So I hardened myself to the noise, and got to the point where the explosions just didn't mean anything.

Then I arrived in Long Bien, Vietnam. We got out of our plane at two in the morning, right in the middle of a mortar attack. We literally had to low-crawl from the plane to a bunker and hide in it until the attack was over. After we'd been processed a couple of hours later, I remember lying down in a temporary barracks. My cot was actually bouncing up and down from the explosions. Even though I'd heard many similar noises in basic training, it suddenly dawned on me that this wasn't friendly fire anymore. Somebody out there was shooting rockets at us, and I was close enough to hear the explosions. As I lay there on that bouncing bunk, I realized, *I'm at war! There's an enemy who is trying to kill me.* That really sobered me up.

Gone was my half-hearted listening to instructions. My instructors didn't have to do anything to get my full attention. When they started the week of training once we arrived—how to adjust to the country, what would be happening, and things like that—I was all ears. The difference was I realized that this was truly life and death. I recognized that I was now in a battle.

Seeds Are Being Planted

Whether you realize it or not, you are now in a battle. Remember, Satan is walking about as a roaring lion, "seeking whom he may devour." The devil is trying to destroy your life today. You could become overwhelmed with that and fearful, but God is also going about seeking who will respond to Him. He's trying to get His anointing, power, and blessings into your life. There's no reason to panic and freeze up in fear, because the Lord is infinitely greater than the devil. However, you do need to sober up and realize that we're in a battle. You can't afford the luxury of indulging your negative emotions and getting into the flesh.

I minister to people all the time who desire the results they see in my life, but aren't willing to do what I do. They want to sit and watch "As the Stomach Turns" on television. They watch R- and X-rated movies, indulging negative emotions that I would never indulge. I recognize that there is a spiritual battle going on, and if I ever began to open up and allow such things into my heart and mind, Satan would take advantage of it. So I live a very restricted life, refraining from many things that other people do. (Ps. 101:3.)

Although many people would like to see blind eyes and deaf ears opened, terminal diseases healed, the dead raised, and financial blessings manifest the way I have (by God's grace), they're not willing to spend the time yielding to and fellowshipping with the Lord in His Word, prayer, and obedience. They'd rather be out in the world, indulging their flesh and thinking, *It's not hurting me to do all of this stuff.* It may not hurt them at that moment, but seeds are being planted.

You can't be tempted with something you don't think. (Heb. 11:15.) If you would quit opening yourself up to envy, strife, division, and all the other negative things our society uses for "entertainment," Satan wouldn't have these inroads into your life.

Mr. Critical

Once I led a man to the Lord who had a pretty rough background. After being born again, he joined our church and began criticizing everything. He criticized people for using soap because it wasn't natural. (He could have used a lot of soap too—he needed it!) He criticized people because they peeled their potatoes, and the skin was the most nutritious part. This guy just had an opinion about everything!

I didn't find out until later, but this fellow had been the first person ever indicted by the California Grand Jury three times before he was a teenager. He had lived in reformatories since the age of five. Because of all this, and growing up around so much strife, there was a tremendous amount of anger and resentment in him.

After a couple of months, he came to me one day and said, "I'm leaving this church. I'm going back out into the desert because there's too much strife here."

I just got bold and told him, "Yes, there is strife in this church, but it's all coming from you. There wasn't any strife among the members until you came in here and started criticizing everybody. You're the source of this strife!"

"Really? I didn't realize it."

"You didn't realize that when you criticize people over everything they do that they aren't going to like that?"

This brother just sat down and began to tell me about his background. Then he said, "I guess I just didn't realize it was strife. I just thought it was normal." Then he continued, saying, "If you were to tell me to act healed when I feel sick, I can do that because I've felt healed before. But when you're telling me to walk in love, I guess I don't know how to do that. I've never felt love before." I had to take this guy and start teaching him through the life of Jesus what it's like to love people.

Some folks come from a background where screaming, yelling, and throwing things were normal. There are plenty of families like that, but it's not the way God wants us to be. (James 3:16.)

Viper in Your House?

Do you treat strangers better than your own family? Many people wouldn't dare to treat me the way that they treat their own children, yet they wonder, *Why am I having these problems with my kids?* Yell at me, "Go make your bed you lousy kid!" scream at me, "Why haven't you done this yet?" and see how our relationship gets along. If that's how you treat your family, you have a double standard.

When you blast your family members—the people you're supposed to love more than anybody else—it's no wonder you're dealing with rebellion, strife, and division. If you want godly relationships, you have to start guarding your tongue. You have to realize that you can't tolerate such strife. Satan comes in through the doors of envy and strife and works every evil work in your life.

Would you allow a poisonous snake to run loose in your house? If it got into the heating vent, perhaps you wouldn't see it for a week or two, but if you knew it was still lurking there, somewhere, you'd probably say, "I don't care how long it takes, I am not going to live in a house with a dangerous, venomous viper on the loose!" It might not be an immediate threat, but if you never knew just where it was…hunting….

Strife is much more deadly than a poisonous snake! Along with envy, strife opens up an inroad for every evil work in your life. It's time you snap out of complacency and recognize that you're in a spiritual battle. You can't tolerate envy, strife, unforgiveness or any other negative emotion.

Some people look at pornographic images and think, *Well, I'll never act that out.* Every time you indulge your flesh, you are releasing spiritual powers into your life. As you give more and more of a place to the devil, I guarantee that it will cost you something. Sin will take you further than you want to go, cost you more than you want to pay, and keep you longer than you want to stay.

Every one of us is exposed to the forces of the kingdom of darkness each and every day. We aren't on R&R (rest and relaxation). We aren't in a secured area where our actions don't really count. We're in a spiritual battle, with a real enemy who wants to take advantage of us any way he can.

Raised From the Dead

God's Word says, "Neither give place to the devil," (Eph. 4:27). You are the one who gives Satan inroads into your life. He takes whatever "place" you give him through your thoughts, words, emotions, and actions.

Your emotions can give Satan a place. Perhaps every once in a while you feel like you should just give in and let your guard down. It would just feel good to have a pity party.

I've felt that way before. One night my older son called on the telephone and told me that my younger son had died. Immediately, my wife and I agreed in prayer, spoke our faith, and commanded him to come back to life. As we got dressed and drove the hour into Colorado Springs, I had some negative emotions. I felt like, *How long can you stand? How long can you be strong? Every once in a while you just need to run up the white flag of surrender and let it out. Why not just gripe and complain?* However, I knew that if I started speaking forth my fears and unbelief that it would have negated my faith. Even though I felt like saying, "We lost this one. We're beaten. Let's give it up and quit," I started building myself up and speaking positive words like, "He will not die, but live and declare the works of the Lord," and "You're a good God. I love You!"

All the glory to Jesus, we arrived in Colorado Springs at the hospital to discover that God had raised him from the dead. He had been dead for almost five hours, but about five minutes or so after we received that phone call from my older son, my younger son just sat up and started talking right there on the slab in the hospital morgue. Praise Jesus!

I firmly believe that if I had given in to and vented my negative emotions, we wouldn't have seen the victory. If I had spoken forth my frustration and complained, saying, "It's not fair," my son wouldn't have been raised from the dead. Satan will take advantage of whatever we give him. We are often hung by our own tongue.

CHAPTER 4

No Wicked Thing

There are times in life when we just feel like speaking forth our negative thoughts and emotions. In light of the spiritual battle, however, these are times we must exercise our faith and self-control.

In Matthew 6:31, the Lord reveals to us at what point we take a thought for our own:

> Take no thought, saying…

A thought becomes your own when you begin speaking it out of your mouth.

You can't keep all kinds of thoughts from coming across your mind. When I found out my son was dead, thoughts of grief, fear, and panic crossed my mind. I'm human, just like anybody else. Yet, you can keep from taking those thoughts as your own.

Kenneth E. Hagin[1] used to say you can't keep a bird from flying over your head, but you can keep it from landing there and building a nest. Negative thoughts will come at times, but you don't have to receive them. They don't have to become a part of you. If you don't say it, it won't be yours.

Hung by the Tongue

Satan passes thoughts, feelings, and attitudes across our hearts and minds. So how do we prevent these seeds from taking root, beginning to grow, and then producing the negative crop he desires? We just saw how—we "take no thought, saying."

If you don't say it, then it's not yours. However, the moment you start verbalizing and speaking forth these negative things, they become yours and begin releasing this negative power in your life. You need to take on this attitude: "I refuse to speak forth anything contrary to what I'm believing for."

Some people are believing for healing. They've asked God to heal them and they're confessing "I believe I'm healed," despite the fact that they haven't seen the physical manifestation yet. But when someone calls them on the phone and asks, "How are you doing?" they respond by telling the person how bad they feel. Without realizing it, they have just released a negative spiritual force.

> Death *and* life are in the power of the tongue.
>
> PROVERBS 18:21

You can't only just speak life with your tongue. You can also speak death. Sadly, the truth is that most of us release much more death than life. We counter ourselves with our own words. We're hung by the tongue!

Words Are Important

You may be praying for one thing and then speaking against it. You may be praying for restoration in your marriage, yet you constantly criticize, beat down, and speak negatively about your marriage on the other hand. You are releasing a negative spiritual force—death—that will counter what you're praying for. Even though God wants to move on your behalf and restore, you're releasing a contrary spiritual force with those negative words.

You need to be careful how you speak about your children. It's not wrong to state a fact. If somebody asks, don't say, "Everything is perfect" when it isn't. You can say, "There are problems *but*..." and then counter it with what you're believing for. It's okay to say, "Here's the problem, *but* everything will work out." On the other hand, if you say, "I'm believing God for a miracle, *but*..." and then you start examining and explaining all of the bad things, you've just destroyed what you're trying to accomplish. It really does matter where you put your *but*.

Sometimes you just have to acknowledge the facts, "Hey, I've got a problem. I'm fighting this sickness..." But then you counter it with the truth of God's Word, "But I believe I'm healed, in Jesus' name."

You need to be constantly aware of the truth that your words are either releasing life or releasing death. Don't just allow anything to come out of your mouth. Set a watch over your mouth and speak life (Ps. 141:3), because you will eat the fruit of it.

> A man's belly shall be satisfied with the fruit of his mouth; and with the increase of his lips shall he be filled.
>
> PROVERBS 18:20

Every word you say out of your mouth is a seed that produces after its kind. If you are griping, complaining, and speaking forth all this negativity, then that's the kind of fruit you'll wind up eating from those words. If you are bitter in your heart, it started with you speaking forth some things that you shouldn't have said. You can't keep a problem from coming, but you can keep those problems from dominating you by speaking forth the right, positive, Word-oriented things. Your words are important!

Blinded to the Truth

In this spiritual battle, Satan takes advantage of the words we say.

> For by thy words thou shalt be justified, and by thy words thou shalt be condemned.
>
> MATTHEW 12:37

When we don't realize just how important our words are, we speak forth foolishness, doubt, unbelief, and other things that allow Satan to devour us because we let down our guard. Part of Paul's commission from God, and ours as well, is to...

> Turn them...from the *power* of Satan unto God.
>
> ACTS 26:18

Many people don't really recognize that Satan is dominating—exerting power in—their lives. They just think it is circumstances, fate, or luck. This scripture makes it very clear that they have been under the influence of the devil.

> You hath he quickened, who were dead in trespasses and sins; wherein in time past ye walked according to the course of this world, according to the prince of the power of the air, the spirit that now worketh in the children of disobedience: among whom also we all had our conversation in times past in the lusts of our flesh, fulfilling the desires of the flesh and of the mind; and were by nature the children of wrath, even as others.
>
> EPHESIANS 2:1–3

Before we converted to Christ, we were by nature children of Satan. We lived our lives under his influence and dominion, blinded to the truth.

> In whom the god of this world hath blinded the minds of them which believe not, lest the light of the glorious gospel of Christ, who is the image of God, should shine unto them.
>
> 2 CORINTHIANS 4:4

The devil is actively at work today hardening people and blinding them from the truths of the Gospel. This is not a passive battle. He's aggressively pursuing and trying to destroy people. One of the reasons why the enemy has such a stronghold on so many people is that the church hasn't really recognized the spiritual battle we're in.

Corrupting Good Manners

As a minister of the Gospel, I use daily programs on both television and radio to share the truth of God's Word all around the world. However, many of the other programs people watch and listen to on television and radio are used of the devil to strengthen his influence and control. Both nonbelievers and Christians alike are plugged into them and, to one degree or another, are fed a steady diet of ungodliness—sexual immorality, violence, strife, hatred, and sarcasm. We allow this sewage to pour into our homes and Satan uses it in our lives. It's not that television or radio are evil in and of themselves. God is using both of them mightily to advance His kingdom. The problem is that Satan also uses the vast majority of their programming—not to build up but to destroy people's lives.

Some folks think, *Oh, I can watch this stuff and it doesn't affect me.* God's Word says they're deceived.

> Be not deceived: evil communications corrupt good manners.
>
> 1 CORINTHIANS 15:33

You may convince yourself that you're not being influenced or corrupted, but the Word reveals otherwise. You simply cannot maintain your spiritual equilibrium while indulging your eyes on ungodliness.

David—the man after God's own heart—understood this. He said:

> I will set no wicked thing before mine eyes.
>
> PSALM 101:3

As a follower of the Lord Jesus Christ, you need to make the same commitment, saying, "I will not watch anything wicked. I refuse to paint a picture on the inside of me of lust, anger, immorality, hatred, strife, or murder. I recognize that every time I open myself up to such things, there is a negative spiritual power there waiting to gain an inroad into my life. By God's grace, I will not give the devil any access into my life!"

Painting Pictures

One of the reasons we have so much violence and immorality in our society is that there's so much violence and immorality on television and in movies. These images are painting pictures in the hearts and minds of people, who are then going out and acting on them. We can't be tempted by what we don't think (Heb. 11:15), but what we think about constantly will become what we talk about and do.

Everything you say and/or do is releasing either God's or Satan's power in your life. Your enemy is an active force at work in the world seeking whom he may devour. (1 Peter 5:8.) He blinds the minds of those who don't believe in order to steal, kill, and destroy them. (2 Cor. 4:4; John 10:10.) Just putting your head in the sand and saying, "I don't believe we're in a battle. I'm just going to continue on the way I've been," isn't going to change the situation. It just means that you'll be one of the casualties. It's to your advantage to recognize the reality of the fight and make the necessary adjustments in your thinking and lifestyle.

We are responsible to submit to God and resist the devil. (James 4:7.) Our thoughts, emotions, words, and actions are either giving place to God or giving place to the devil. (Eph. 4:27.) We need to recognize the spiritual dynamics happening all around us.

I'm amazed how many people don't associate their actions with the results they're experiencing. They totally miss the correlation and don't have a clue how Satan is destroying them. While living a life in opposition to God, they come up to me and say, "I just don't understand why the devil is after me."

"Are You Married?"

One time I had a man in our church come out to shoe my horse. While he was doing that, we began talking and he kept referring to his "girlfriend." I'd seen him at church with this woman and thought she was his wife. However, the way he kept talking about his girlfriend led me to believe they weren't married. So finally, I just asked him, "Are you married?"

He answered, "Oh no. We're just living together. We've had so many friends that have married and divorced that we think it's wise to live together for a while and see if we should get married or not. It's been about six months now."

Immediately, I asked, "I thought you said you were a Christian?"

"Well, I am. I was born again four months ago."

"Don't you realize that living together is contrary to God's Word?"

This guy was a brand-new believer and totally ignorant of the Scriptures. "You mean God says something about just living with a person before you get married?"

So I started sharing the Word with him. After a little while, he said, "Well, we love each other and we're going to get married. So it'll be okay."

I had to explain to him, "It doesn't matter what's going to happen in the future. Right now you are living in a way that exempts you from God's power. You have yielded yourself to Satan and have violated God's Word. By doing so, you have released demonic power in your life. The devil is just having a heyday with you!"

Follow God's Instructions

As we continued talking, he began to open up his heart. Usually it takes thirty minutes to shoe a horse, but this one took three hours. He was just soaking it up. This brother changed his mind, moved out, and they straightened up their act.

When you disobey God, you open up a door to the devil. Now, contrary to what religion says, God still loves you. He's not mad at you, but He wants better for you. By violating God's instructions in His Word and obeying the lust of your flesh, you've thrown open a door to the devil. Satan will come in, eat your lunch, and pop the bag!

If you don't want that, you may need to change your mind and adjust your actions. We're in a spiritual battle, and you can't afford the luxury of just ignoring the instructions God has given you.

CHAPTER 5

Unconditional Authority

In the previous chapters, I've established that we are in a battle. This isn't something that only some people experience or that will come to us in the future. We are facing a spiritual battle right now, every day. So, we need to define who our enemy is and reveal what power he has.

In almost forty years of being a Christian and actively studying God's Word, I've come across several different opinions about where Satan came from and how he got his power. I've heard all kinds of messages on this subject and, in my personal study, I've read many different commentaries, study Bibles, and books. However, in the midst of these different variations, a dominant doctrine has emerged in popular theology. This widely held understanding says that God created a powerful, beautiful, godly angel named "Lucifer." (Isa. 14:12.) This Lucifer was "the anointed cherub that covereth" on God's holy mountain. (Ezek. 28:14.) Many people believe that he had musical instruments—pipes and tambourines—built into his body. (Ezek. 28:13.) Lucifer was perfect in all his ways. (Ezek. 28:15.) In spite of that, he became prideful, turned into Satan, and rebelled against God.

At this point, popular theology also says that Satan convinced one-third of the angels to follow him in rebellion. Together, they attempted to overthrow God, were defeated, and were then all cast down to the earth. They base this premise upon Revelation 12:4, which is the only scripture in the entire Bible that even makes reference to this. Basing a major doctrine on a single passage of scripture, especially one so full of symbolism, is not good Bible interpretation.

Child Abuse?

Some people take this even further, saying that Satan ruled over a pre-Adamic civilization once he was thrown down from heaven to earth. They argue that God brought a cataclysmic judgment upon the devil and his kingdom, and that the earth was completely destroyed in between Genesis 1:1 ("God created the heaven and the earth") and 1:2 ("The earth was without form, and void"). They propose that Genesis 1:2 is actually the re-creation. Finis Dake, through the extensive notes in his study Bible and commentary, really popularized this theory. This is where many people who teach this point of view today—either directly or indirectly—received their information.

They also say that Satan and his demons came from this pre-Adamic civilization. Once Adam and Eve were created, God allowed Satan—with all of his evilness and corruption—into the Garden of Eden so that man would have a choice between good and evil. That's like saying, "God took His man and put him in the garden with this evil, wild beast just to tempt them and see how they would do."

Most people don't really give serious thought to why things are the way they are. Like life, they just deal with the Bible on a surface level. Have you ever pondered the question, "If God is a good and loving God, then why did He allow Satan to come into the garden and tempt Adam and Eve?" That's comparable to letting your two-year-old child go out in the backyard to play, knowing full well that a hungry lion or bear—something that could literally destroy them—is lurking in the bushes. We'd consider that irresponsible. In the natural realm, we'd take kids away from a parent who didn't take care of and protect their children any better than that. A parent who would knowingly and willingly expose their children to such a dangerous predator—if caught—would be arrested, convicted, and thrown in jail on charges of child abuse. Yet, this popular theology insinuates that our heavenly Father turned Satan loose in the Garden of Eden to tempt Adam and Eve.

I don't believe that's the way it happened at all. Now, the Bible doesn't totally explain why God did what He did with man and Satan, but I believe there are clues. And it's these clues that have led me to some totally different conclusions than what are popularly believed.

Ministering Spirits

God sent Lucifer—His top angel—down to earth to minister to Adam and Eve. Lucifer hadn't transgressed against God—and become Satan—yet. He was a godly angel in the Garden of Eden on special assignment from the Lord Himself.

> Are they [angels] not all ministering spirits, sent forth to minister for them who shall be heirs of salvation?
>
> HEBREWS 1:14

Angels are all sent to minister to us. God didn't send Lucifer to the earth to tempt Adam and Eve, but to serve them and minister to them. He came to the garden on a divine mission. However, once there, he transgressed.

Isaiah 14 and Ezekiel 28 provide us with the vast majority of the Old Testament information that we have about this angel called Lucifer who became Satan. In both passages, the prophet began by addressing a physical person (the king of Babylon—Isa. 14:4; and the king of Tyrus—Ezek. 28:12). Nevertheless, it becomes obvious through the prophet's words (Isa. 14:12; Ezek. 28:13) that the demonic power behind that physical person is really who's being addressed.

Subtle Switch

In the New Testament, Jesus did the same thing when He turned to Peter and said:

> Get thee behind me, Satan: thou art an offence unto me: for thou savourest not the things that be of God, but those that be of men.
>
> MATTHEW 16:23

He was addressing the demonic power operating through the physical human being.

Keep this in mind, and watch for the subtle switch, as we begin looking at this passage of scripture.

> Moreover the word of the LORD came unto me, saying, Son of man, take up a lamentation upon the king of Tyrus [a physical human being], and say unto him.
>
> EZEKIEL 28:11,12

Lucifer's Transgression

Now this next section is clearly speaking to the demonic personality—Satan himself—who was operating through this physical human being. It's obvious because of what the next few verses say.

> Thou hast been in Eden the garden of God; every precious stone was thy covering, the sardius, topaz, and the diamond, the beryl, the onyx, and the jasper, the sapphire, the emerald, and the carbuncle, and gold: the workmanship of thy tabrets and of thy pipes was prepared in

> thee in the day that thou wast created. Thou art the anointed cherub that covereth; and I have set thee so: thou wast upon the holy mountain of God; thou hast walked up and down in the midst of the stones of fire. Thou wast perfect in thy ways from the day that thou wast created, till iniquity was found in thee.
>
> EZEKIEL 28:13–15

This is describing Lucifer, specifically in the Garden of Eden. Notice how it's describing him still in a sinless state. God sent Lucifer—the most honored, and respected angel He created—down to the Garden of Eden to be a servant to mankind.

Lucifer's transgression against God came in the Garden of Eden. It's described in Genesis 3 when he entered into the snake and used this serpent to speak to Eve and tempt her. Then he persuaded both Eve and Adam to eat of the forbidden fruit. That's when Lucifer transgressed against God.

Revelation 12:3–4, where the dragon took one-third of the stars and threw them to the earth, is a flimsy basis for saying that Satan took one-third of the angels and rebelled against God. The devil wouldn't have won if he had 100 percent of the angels, much less only one-third. There's no way Satan could even come close to winning a direct confrontation with God.

No Restrictions

Lucifer came to the earth as an anointed angel on a divine assignment to minister to Adam and Eve. However, he saw something in them that he didn't have. As an angel, his power and authority was conditional (my supposition). But Adam and Eve had been given unconditional power and authority over this earth. We see this where God created Adam and Eve, in the creation story of Genesis 1.

> God said, Let us make man in our image, after our likeness: and *let them have dominion* [power and authority] over the fish of the sea, and over the fowl of the air, and over the cattle, and *over all the earth, and over every creeping thing that creepeth upon the earth.* So God created man in his own image, in the image of God created he him; male and female created he them. And God blessed them, and *God said unto them,* Be fruitful, and multiply, and replenish the earth, and subdue it: and *have dominion* over the fish of the sea, and *over the fowl of the air, and over every living thing that moveth upon the earth.*
>
> GENESIS 1:26–28

When God created man, He spoke and gave them dominion—power and authority—over all the earth. Notice that there were no restrictions placed on this. God didn't say to them, "Now as long as you follow My leading and do what I want you to do, I'll let you have dominion over the earth." No, God placed zero qualifications on this dominion that He gave to mankind.

God's Integrity

Once God speaks, it's done. He never goes back on His Word.

> My covenant will I not break, nor alter the thing that is gone out of my lips.
>
> PSALM 89:34

According to Hebrews 6:18, it is "impossible for God to lie" because:

> God is not a man, that he should lie; neither the son of man, that he should repent: hath he said, and shall he not do it? or hath he spoken, and shall he not make it good?
>
> NUMBERS 23:19

The integrity of God's Word is what makes the universe exist and hold together. God upholds "all things by the word of his power" (Heb. 1:3).

God will not violate what He has said. So when He told Adam and Eve, "You have dominion; you have power and authority over this earth; you rule it and subdue it; it's under your control," He meant it. God gave them dominion over this earth.

Bound by His Word

Of course, the Lord never meant for man to use that power and authority in the way that we did. He didn't mean for us to just turn it over to Satan. However, because of God's own integrity, once we did yield that dominion over to the devil, God couldn't just say, "Time out. King's X. This isn't what I intended. Stop. We're going to do this all over again. I take back this authority. You can't run the earth anymore." That's what we would tend to do if someone abused the privilege we gave them. But that's not how He is. God was bound by His own Word.

Think of it. God has magnified His Word above His name.

> Thou hast magnified thy word above all thy name.
>
> Psalm 138:2

At the name of Jesus—the name which is above all names—every knee will bow and every tongue will confess that He is Lord. (Phil. 2:9–11.) "The name of the Lord is a strong tower" (Prov. 18:10), yet the Word of God is magnified even above the name of Jesus.

Knowing God as he did, Lucifer's antennae went up when he heard the Lord say to Adam and Eve, "You have dominion" without any restrictions or qualifications. That got the top angel's attention because he knew that the God-given authority that he operated in was conditional (again, my supposition). If Lucifer were to disobey God, this divine power that had been delegated to him would have instantly been taken away. He had no ability to use the power that

God had given him to fight against God. There was no chance of Lucifer directly rebelling at God. But perhaps he could rebel if somehow he could get a hold of that unconditional power and authority that had been given to man.

I admit that some of these things aren't clearly spelled out in Scripture. We may indeed be bumping up against some things that are beyond our ability to know.

> The secret things belong unto the LORD our God: but those things which are revealed belong unto us and to our children for ever.
>
> DEUTERONOMY 29:29

God hasn't revealed every single thing to us. Yet, from what I do know of God's nature, character, and Word, the evidence points strongly in this direction.

An Opportunity

The Bible reveals that angels also have a free will.

> God spared not the angels that sinned, but cast them down to hell, and delivered them into chains of darkness, to be reserved unto judgment.
>
> 2 PETER 2:4

Although angels have a free will, there's no reason to believe that their power and authority is unconditional like Adam and Eve's. Therefore, if any angels got out of line, God could, in a sense, just fire them. He could cancel and recall the power and authority He had given them, and they'd be absolutely defeated.

In light of this, there's no way Satan and one-third of the angels could charge God on His throne, who still retained two-thirds of the angels. However, Lucifer saw an opportunity with the unconditional authority over the earth that God had given to mankind.

CHAPTER 6

God of This World

The Lord made Adam and Eve the gods of this world.

> I have said, Ye are gods; and all of you are children of the most High.
>
> PSALM 82:6

In context, this was God creating man and saying to him, "You are gods." This isn't "Gods" in the sense of divinity, but "gods" in the sense of rulership. We were given dominion—power and authority—over the earth. Since it was ours to rule and reign, we were gods over this earth.

> The heaven, even the heavens, are the LORD's: but the earth hath he given to the children of men.
>
> PSALM 115:16

God literally gave the earth to mankind. The Creator gave us the power and authority to rule over this earth as if we were the creator. We weren't the Creator, but that's how much dominion He gave us.

"I Will..."

I believe that when Lucifer—still the sinless, perfect angel of God in the garden sent to minister to Adam and Eve—saw the unconditional authority over the earth that God had given to man, he recognized an opportunity. Isaiah 14 reveals his thought process.

> O Lucifer, son of the morning...thou hast said in thine heart, *I will* ascend into heaven, *I will* exalt my throne above the stars of God: *I will* sit also upon the mount of the congregation, in the sides of the north: *I will* ascend above the heights of the clouds: *I will* be like the most High.
>
> ISAIAH 14:12–14

Lucifer envied God. He wasn't content with being the top angel. He was jealous and wanted God's position, but he couldn't just take that place with the delegated power he had been given. If he would have rebelled, that power would have instantly been taken away and he would have been destroyed. However, he saw an opportunity with man because God had given Adam and Eve something that He'd never given to the angels—an unconditional, no reservations or qualifications, no strings attached authority over the earth. Lucifer saw that if he could get Adam and Eve to yield to him and rebel against God, then he could become the new "god" of this world. (2 Cor. 4:4.)

Even though the Bible hadn't been written down yet, Lucifer knew that the Word of God was settled from the beginning (Ps. 119:89), and that the Lord never changes. (Mal. 3:6.) Therefore, creation has always operated under God's unchangeable spiritual laws, which include:

> Know ye not, that to whom ye yield yourselves servants to obey, his servants ye are to whom ye obey; whether of sin unto death, or of obedience unto righteousness?
>
> ROMANS 6:16

Understanding how God's kingdom works, Lucifer knew that if he could trick Adam and Eve into yielding to and obeying him, then he could become their master. Then he could take the power and authority that had been given to mankind and use it to begin thwarting the kingdom of God and start receiving the praise, adoration, and glory that he desired. That's how it happened.

Taken Hostage

When someone robs a bank, they sometimes take a hostage. A bank usually has all kinds of powerful security—locks, alarms, vaults, cameras, and armed guards. One person with a gun isn't really sufficient to go in and overpower all of that security. In spite of this, if the thief grabs a hostage and puts a gun to the hostage's head, the thief knows his or her demands will be met. The people who run the bank aren't willing to see a hostage killed just to protect some money. So, one person with a gun and six bullets can challenge the far greater force of multiple guards with automatic weapons and several cartridges each. Technically, the thief shouldn't be able to overpower the security. But with a hostage, the thief is able to get away with the robbery.

Satan knew he couldn't overpower God in a direct confrontation. However, he saw how God gave Adam and Eve an unconditional authority. If they of their own free will yielded to him, they would also transfer that authority over to him as well.

As Creator and owner, God could have come down and wiped out the world. He could have destroyed Adam and Eve, the devil, and all of the angels that rebelled. As Creator, He had the right to do that and start over. Yet, to intervene in the affairs of this world like that would have violated His Word. He had given the dominion over this earth to Adam and Eve. He had given the power and authority to rule over this world to physical human beings. If God would have intervened, He would have violated His Word, and the entire universe would have self-destructed because it's held together by the integrity of His Word. (Heb. 1:3.)

For God to maintain His integrity and stand by what He had previously said—"You have dominion"—He had to give Adam and Eve their freedom. If they wanted to yield their authority and power over the earth to Satan, then technically it was their right to do so. God would have been unjust to come down here, destroy Satan, say, "Adam and Eve, don't do this again," and then redeem them. He couldn't do that and still be faithful to the Word He had spoken over them. They had a choice.

Lucifer saw how much God loved Adam and Eve. He met with them every day in the cool of the evening. (Gen. 3:8.) After creating the whole universe—billions and billions of galaxies, stars, and planets—God was bound to have other things to do, yet He spent time with Adam and Eve every single day. So Satan gambled that God wouldn't come down and wipe out this creation that He'd made.

Satan Needs Submission

Satan was using Adam and Eve as hostages to hide behind, saying, "God, they gave me this authority. It was their choice. I didn't force them." Satan didn't come as a mammoth and put his foot on Eve's head. He didn't come and overpower them. The devil came with deception, and they willingly yielded to him. This is where his transgression took place—in the Garden of Eden. He used them like a hostage, saying, "God, if You want to do anything to me, you'll have to destroy Adam and Eve too. They did this of their own free will."

Due to God's great love for mankind, Satan was allowed to become god of this world. Instead of wiping us out and starting this whole thing over, God allowed what we did to stand. *We are the ones who made Satan.* We are the ones who enabled Lucifer to leave his position in heaven, come into a fallen state, and rule the earth as Satan—the god of this world.

We were originally intended to be gods—absolute rulers—over this world. But mankind gave their dominion—authority and power—to Lucifer. So God created Lucifer, but Adam and Eve made Satan. They didn't create Satan in the sense that God had already created Lucifer as an angelic being. Adam and Eve *made* Satan who he was by giving him their power and authority.

Most people believe that Satan is using a superior power and authority to oppress mankind. They see him as this huge, powerful being who is so much superior to any of us. This is reflected in television shows and horror movies. Satan and his demons are portrayed as these strong, powerful beings. Most people see the devil as a superior being in power and authority.

They don't understand that Lucifer lost his divinely delegated, God-given power the very instant he transgressed and became Satan. The devil is not using a superior power and authority against us. He's actually using the same power and authority that God gave mankind to rule and reign with over this earth. It's our own power and authority that he uses against us.

On his own, Satan is powerless. He depends completely on physical human beings yielding to and empowering him. Even under the Old Covenant, Satan didn't have the power to control and dominate people. He has to use our own power and authority against us. It's only as we submit to him that Satan is able to do anything.

A Demon Needs a Body

The devil and his demons—as spirit beings—have no power or authority on this earth apart from physical human beings yielding it to them.

Consider the example of Jesus casting out the demons in Luke 8. When the Lord commanded the unclean spirit out of a man, the demons identified themselves as "Legion" because they were many. (Luke 8:30.) They begged Jesus, "Don't cast us out into the deep, but send us into that nearby herd of swine." When the demons entered these 2,000 pigs, this herd immediately took off running, jumped off a steep cliff, and drowned themselves in a lake. (vv. 31–33.)

Demons are looking for a physical body, a willing vessel. They need somebody who will submit to them. The power that the devil or any other demon uses against us is our own. Satan has zero angelic, spiritual power. All his authority comes from man. The only reason Satan exists and functions is because people cooperate with and empower him. That's why he always seeks to inhabit a body. Even a pig has more authority on earth than a demon. An ant, a fly, or a snail has more power on this earth than Satan because they have physical bodies. He is absolutely powerless to do anything unless he can get a physical body to cooperate with him.

The Right to Use Power

God is the author of all power and authority. When He created mankind, He gave Adam and Eve dominion over the earth. (Gen. 1:26–28.) God gave us—physical human beings—power and authority to rule this world. Authority is simply the right to use power. God gave that right to use power to Adam and Eve. Basically, God said, "Here's My power. Now I give you the right to use My power. Everything I have created will respond to you."

God is a Spirit. (John 4:24.) Satan is a spirit too. (Eph. 2:2.) He doesn't have a physical body, which means that he can't come and make anyone do anything. First, he must gain their cooperation.

Many Christians see Satan as an angelic being with godlike supernatural power and authority over man. They see him coming and overpowering them, when the truth is that the devil can't force them to do anything. He lost his power when he rebelled at God. The only power and authority Satan is functioning under now is human power and authority.

It takes your cooperation for the devil to do anything in your life. That's why he seeks whom he *may* devour. Satan doesn't have the authority and power to devour you unless you quit obeying God and yield yourself to sin. Romans 6:16 says that when you yield yourself to sin, you're actually yielding yourself to the author of that sin, which is Satan. Satan can't just come in and destroy you without your cooperation. But when you sin, you are empowering the devil.

Earthsuits

Most people don't see it this way. They understand that, according to Scripture, Satan was originally created as an angel. Angels have a higher power than what we do, but they don't have the authority—the right—to exercise that power in the earth. Yet, most people assume that Satan has a higher power and authority than us, and they are intimidated by that perceived authority. They don't realize that he lost all of his angelic power when he rebelled, and now his authority is totally tied to us. Since God gave the authority over this earth and everything going on in it, to physical human beings, Satan—who is without a physical body—is absolutely powerless unless we empower him by yielding to and indulging his lust, lies, anger, bitterness, unforgiveness, or some other sin.

This is why our actions are so important. Your physical body is what gives you authority here on the earth. Paul the apostle doesn't have any power or influence over you today. He's still alive, but he's no longer in a physical body. The only influence he has on anyone today is through the physical writings he left behind. People can read them and be influenced. Nevertheless, Paul doesn't have the authority to function and operate any longer on this earth because he no longer has a physical body. I have a physical body. I have more authority and power on this earth than the apostle Paul right now because he has lost his earthsuit. This earthsuit—my physical body—is what empowers me and gives me authority.

Satan can't do anything without somebody in an earthsuit yielding to him. This is why he's constantly vying for your heart, trying to get you to yield to him through anger, fear, hurt, pain, and depression. Every time you move away from what God's Word says and act in union with what the devil is trying to do, you yield authority to him. Every time you quit believing and receiving God's supernatural power and ability and sin instead, you empower the enemy. Satan can only function as he keeps people submitted to himself through lies and deception.

It's sad to say, but one of his greatest weapons of deception has been the church. The church has taught that Satan is a superior power. He isn't. He's actually using nothing but human power and human authority acquired through our cooperation.

My Own Human Authority

Does that mean Satan isn't a factor? No, he is a factor. There are millions of people on the face of the earth who are yielded to the devil today. They are operating in sexual immorality, lies, deception, hurt, fear, hatred, idolatry, and more. Every time we yield to something negative, we empower the devil. So, yes, Satan is a factor and he has to be dealt with.

But as far as my individual life goes, Satan can't do anything without my consent and cooperation. Understanding that the power and authority Satan uses is human power—the power God has given to me, a physical human being, to rule and reign over this earth—has put everything in a brand-new light.

Now, instead of being intimidated by the enemy, I have boldness toward the devil. I understand that if I were to start doing the wrong things in my actions, saying the wrong things with my words, and indulging negative emotions, Satan would take advantage of it. He'd come in, eat my lunch, and pop the bag. I'm not ignorant of his devices, but I'm also not afraid of him. I'm not being passive toward him, but I'm actively and intentionally resisting him. I realize that all he's doing is coming against me with my own human authority and power.

I received a testimony from a woman who had been a Satanist before converting to Christ. Even after being born again, she suffered many problems because she was afraid that Satan was mad at her and was trying to punish her for turning away from him. When she heard this teaching on the believer's authority, it set her free. All her fears left as she realized that the devil couldn't do anything to her without her consent and cooperation. These truths liberated this precious sister, and they'll liberate you too!

CHAPTER 7

Under the Umbrella

In light of what we've seen thus far, Ephesians 6:10–11 ought to make a lot more sense.

> Finally, my brethren, be strong in the Lord, and in the power of his might. Put on the whole armour of God, that ye may be able to stand against the wiles of the devil.

Wiles literally means "cunningness, craftiness, and deception."[1] Satan's only power is deception. He can't force you to do anything. He can't make you sin. People tell me, "I don't want to commit sexual sin, but I just don't have the power to resist. Satan is stronger than I am." Not true. Satan doesn't have the power or the authority to force you to do anything. The problem is that he's a master liar, intimidator, and deceiver. It's all deception. When we don't know the truth about who we are in Christ and the power we've been given, then—in a very real sense—we are the ones who are giving Satan the power and authority to rule and dominate us. You can break that.

Recently I was speaking to one of our Bible college students about a certain area in the student's life, and that person admitted, "I know I'm wrong in this area. It's rebellion and I want to break it, but there's just something in me that I have trouble doing the right thing. I just can't seem to overcome it."

I told the student, "Here's how you can overcome it. Do what you know you're supposed to do but don't feel like doing, every day. It doesn't matter that you don't feel like doing it. Do it every day. If you'll start obeying and yielding your actions to the Lord, then He'll be strengthened in your life. As you quit obeying and yielding your body to the devil, it'll weaken him in your life." That's why the Bible says you have to stand against the wiles, deception, lies, and deceit of the devil.

Satan is out to deceive you and he's coming at you every which way through all of the help and support he gets from people. Our airwaves are full of lust and lies. Every time you yield to the lies, you are the one who empowers the devil to come in and destroy your life.

Why Jesus Came

Since God is a Spirit and doesn't have a physical body (John 4:24), and since He gave the power and authority over the earth to physical human beings, He would have been unjust to come down here and intervene in the affairs of man. He couldn't just step in and straighten out the mess. He had the power to do so, and as Judge He could have said, "Alright, I'm tired of this whole mess. I'm going to wipe out the entire human race."

He came close to doing that with Noah and the flood. As Creator and owner, He's always had the right and privilege, but outside of total judgment, He didn't have the authority to just come into the affairs of men and change things. He didn't have it because He had given that authority to rule and reign over the earth to mankind. (Ps. 115:16.) Even though they used that authority in a way contrary to what He desired, God would have been unjust and untrue to His own statements to come down here and change things.

This is why God had to become a man. This is the reason that God had to send His Son, the Lord Jesus Christ, to this earth. It all comes back to this issue of authority being given to physical human beings. God didn't have a physical human body, so He wasn't free to just operate unrestricted on this earth. He had to become a man. Jesus—the Word made flesh, the God-Man—had to become a physical person so that He could have authority on this earth. (John 1:14.)

God couldn't have saved mankind any other way. Until He obtained a physical human body, He was limited in what He could do. He tried to work through people, but they were all corrupted, deceived, and under the devil's control.

> I sought for a man among them, that should make up the hedge, and stand in the gap before me for the land, that I should not destroy it: but I found none.
>
> Ezekiel 22:30

> He saw that there was no man, and wondered that there was no intercessor: therefore his arm brought salvation unto him; and his righteousness, it sustained him.
>
> Isaiah 59:16

Since there was no person sinless, pure, and able to bring God's righteousness into the earth, He had to come and save us Himself. He had given the dominion of this world to physical human beings, so He had to become one. God Himself took upon Himself flesh, and limited Himself to a physical body. My teaching entitled "How to Conceive a Miracle" goes into greater depth on this topic. It's the second message from *Lessons From the Christmas Story.*

Four Thousand Years

God spoke Adam's body into existence when He had absolute authority over the earth.

> God said, Let us make man.
>
> GENESIS 1:26

God created man by speaking words. Subsequently, He spoke words giving man dominion—authority and power—over the earth. In doing so, He limited His own authority. Man corrupted themselves by selling out to the devil and making him the god of this world. God wasn't in control. He didn't have dominion over the earth because He had given it to man.

That's why God wasn't able to just speak the physical body of Jesus into existence on His own. He had to speak to the spirits of men—the corrupted spirit within them—and then they had to take those words and speak them out of their mouths. It literally took God four thousand years to find enough people who would operate in enough faith to speak forth and prophesy the things that needed to be spoken for Jesus' body to be created. There's no telling how many people God inspired to say, "A virgin shall conceive, and bear a son" before Isaiah actually spoke it (Isa. 7:14). Not many prophets would like to stand up and go on record declaring such a thing. It took a lot of faith for Isaiah to say that.

After all of these prophecies had been spoken over four thousand years, the angel approached Mary and told her what would happen. (Luke 1:28–33, 35.) She humbled herself and said:

> Behold the handmaid of the Lord; be it unto me according to thy word.
>
> LUKE 1:38

The angel took all of those prophecies—the spoken words of God—and the Word entered into Mary's womb.

> The Word was made flesh, and dwelt among us.
>
> JOHN 1:14

God created the physical body for Jesus to inhabit by speaking words over a four thousand year period of time through anointed men. Then those words entered into the womb of Mary, and that's how Jesus was conceived.[2] That's why He had authority on earth to do what He did.

Shielded From the Rain

Satan was in trouble now. God always had the power to intervene, but He had given the authority over the earth to mankind. His ability to intervene in the affairs of man was limited because He didn't have a physical body. When man turned from God and gave their authority and power to the devil, he began to oppress the human race. God wanted to redeem us, but He had to have some physical human being—a person with a physical body—here on the earth so that He could have authority to do battle with the devil.

When you're under an umbrella, it shields you from the rain. The rain may be falling, but it isn't touching you. When Satan rebelled against God by deceiving men and gaining their authority, he came under the protective "umbrella" of the authority God had given to mankind. This human authority shielded the devil from God getting to him and stripping him of all this power. God couldn't get to Satan directly without violating His Word because He had given authority over the earth to people with physical human bodies. This is why Jesus had to become a Man.

Christ said it this way:

> For as the Father hath life in himself; so hath he given to the Son to have life in himself; and hath given him authority to execute judgment also, because he is the Son of man.
>
> JOHN 5:26,27

Jesus said the reason He had authority to execute judgment was because He was the Son of Man.

The God-Man

Both of the terms "Son of God" and "Son of Man" refer to Jesus. *Son of Man* emphasizes His humanity and physical side. *Son of God* emphasizes His divinity and the presence of Almighty God that indwelt Christ's body. Jesus existed before the worlds began and He created all things. (Col. 1:16–17.) Jesus was God manifest in the flesh. (1 Tim. 3:16.) He was fully God and fully man simultaneously. Therefore, Jesus was the God-Man.

Son of Man refers to Christ's humanity. So when Jesus said that the Father had given Him authority to execute judgment because He was the Son of Man, He was making a direct reference to the fact that He had a physical body. He always had power as Creator, but He didn't have the authority to use that power until He took on flesh.

All this confirms the integrity of God's Word. Once He spoke, "You have dominion" to mankind, it was theirs. He limited His own authority and power on the earth by giving it to us, and God never breaks His Word.

One time one of my employees was believing God for a car. When the Lord blessed me with a better vehicle, I gave my previous car to this person. It was a very nice car. It was brand-new when I got it, and my wife and I had only used it for a couple of years. I gave this car to my employee as a gift and signed the title over to him.

A year or so later, he asked if it would be okay with me if he used that car as a trade-in toward a better one. I told him, "You can do anything you want with that car. It's not mine, it's yours." He felt he needed to get my permission, but it wasn't necessary. In every way I had given him that car. It was legally his. If he wanted to park it on the curb and charge ten dollars each for people to take a swing at it with a sledgehammer in order to raise money for another car, he could have done so. He could have done anything with it he wanted.

That's integrity. If I gave someone a car and signed it over to them, it's theirs. If a couple of years later I find them selling swings with a sledgehammer for ten bucks each and that's not what I intended, it would be wrong for me to come up to them and say something. If I truly gave the car to them—no strings attached—then it's their business, not mine. They now have the authority over it.

A Physical Body

That's how God gave authority over this earth to us. God Himself was limited until He became a physical human being. Jesus wasn't only physical, but He—God Himself—inhabited a physical body on the earth. Now the devil was in trouble. He'd been using Adam and Eve like a hostage, saying, "God, if You do anything to me, You'll have to destroy these people You have made too." But now Jesus became one of the hostages—a physical human being.

Jesus entered into the devil's kingdom and destroyed it. He took away all authority and power from Satan and reduced him to a zero with the rim knocked off. The enemy has zip, zilch, nada power and authority against us. All Satan can do is tempt us. If we yield to him, we're doing the same thing Adam and Eve did—*we* are yielding *our* human power and authority. Satan can't do anything to you without your consent and cooperation.

This is completely opposite of so much of what the church has taught. Most people think that Satan is a major force to be reckoned with. He does exist, and you can't just be ignorant of his devices. (2 Cor. 2:11.) You need to know what's going on, but the devil is not someone to be feared. He's someone you need to recognize and resist, but Satan can't do anything to you without your consent and cooperation.

Understanding this truth has transformed my life and given me a tremendous advantage over the devil. Now I recognize that if I'm having a feeling, a desire, a drawing, or a lust in some direction, all I have to do is quit yielding to those things that are allowing Satan to draw me in that way. I just use my physical body to go in exactly the opposite direction. What I do with my physical body releases either the power of God or the power of the devil.

CHAPTER 8

Is This the One?

When Jamie and I first started out in the ministry, we really struggled financially. Occasionally, I'd work odd jobs to help make ends meet. One day I came home from a painting job feeling so sick that I could hardly stand up. I just wanted to lie down on the couch and rest. Jamie was in the kitchen fixing me lunch. When she saw me on the couch, she asked, "What are you doing?"

"I feel sick. I don't know if I can eat anything."

We had already been teaching other believers these same truths we've mentioned so far: "You have to use your body to quit yielding to the devil. Don't cooperate with him. Do the very thing that you don't feel like doing. Resist the devil, and fight against him with your physical actions." (James 4:7.)

Jamie came right over and got me up off of that couch. She put my arm around her shoulder and started dragging me through the house, saying, "We need this money. You will go back to that job. You're healed!" She made me get up and start acting healed. She just forced me to practice what I'd been preaching.

Praise God, in ten minutes I was over it and felt well again. I went back to work and got paid that day.

"Act on the Word!"

The night before I was to be ordained into the ministry, I hurt my back opening our broken garage door. We were living in Seagoville, Texas, at the time. As I bent over and started lifting up the garage door, it got caught and something just popped in my back. The pain that immediately shot through my body was so excruciating that it knocked me to the ground.

My one-year-old son had been watching me. I told him, "Go tell Mommy," but he just sat there jabbering at me. Eventually, he wandered into the house and brought Jamie out. When she saw me lying there, I hurt so bad that all I could do was whisper, "I hurt my back."

"Well then, get up." Jamie pulled me up, prayed over me, and said, "Now, you act on the Word of God!" Again, we needed me to be able to work, so she cut me no slack.

I started doing things with my physical body. My shoulder blades were back so far they were touching each other. The pain was excruciating, but I forced myself to do things I didn't feel like doing. Finally, over a day's period of time, I got to where I could do sit-ups and other things. Although my movement had returned, my shoulders were still pulled back.

I went to bed that night and woke up on the day I was scheduled to be ordained. My shoulders were still pulled back, but I just kept fighting it all day long. Right before I went to my ordination service, I declared, "I am going to act healed. I am going there, and I will be ordained." By the time I arrived at church, I was healed. My actions played a major part in receiving and manifesting that healing.

You can't lie in bed acting sick and at the same time release the supernatural power of God. You must learn how to use your physical body to resist the devil and cooperate with the Lord. If you don't step out in faith and act on the Word, you'll limit God. (James 2:20.)

We Can Limit God

We've seen that God is a Spirit and that He gave dominion over this earth to physical human beings. (Gen. 1:26–28.) In doing so, He limited His own dominion and authority. If we don't cooperate with God, we can limit Him.

> Yea, they turned back and tempted God, and limited the Holy One of Israel.
>
> PSALM 78:41

Yes, we can limit God. Jesus dealt with this in His own hometown.

> He could there do no mighty work…because of their unbelief.
>
> MARK 6:5,6

It's not that Jesus didn't want to; He couldn't do any mighty work because of their unbelief. Even the Lord Jesus Christ had to have cooperation from people to release His power into their lives.

Religion says, "God is sovereign. He controls everything." No, He doesn't. God is sovereign, in the sense that He's King of kings, but He doesn't control everything that happens on the earth. God isn't limited in the sense that He doesn't have the power. He has the power, but He gave dominion over this earth to physical human beings. Because of His own integrity, He will not overstep that authority and violate His own Word.

Therefore, God has limited His own sovereignty, His own ability to intervene in the affairs of man here on earth. Until He became a physical being Himself, He didn't have the authority to come down to this earth and straighten out the mess man had created.

For additional study on this topic, I recommend, *The Sovereignty of God, Taking the Limits Off God,* and *Spiritual Authority.* They all go into further detail than I can right here.

Earn the Right

God Himself operates within these laws of authority. He will not violate His own Word.

Because we live in a culture today where authority isn't a big issue, these truths can be hard to comprehend. People basically don't submit themselves to authority. They only do what they are forced and demanded to do, but they don't recognize authority. People violate authority all the time.

I don't mean this in a critical way, but the younger generation as a whole doesn't respect authority the way the older generation does. They've been raised in such a way that they believe they can get away with anything. They see little wrong with cheating. They aren't submitted to authority. They think as long as they don't get caught, everything is fine. That's absolutely wrong. All of life is based on authority.

I teach our Charis Bible College students that you have to earn the right to speak into someone's life. You have to gain their respect before they'll let you minister to their heart. This works on every level.

One reason so much of what's called "evangelism" today isn't very effective is that it's disrespectful and offensive. Some Christians just walk up to a stranger, stick a religious tract in their face, and say, "You're going to hell. Repent!" Then they try to coerce that person to submit to them, and "pray a prayer," however, they haven't even had the common courtesy to introduce themselves or ask, "How are you? How's your day going?" These so-called "evangelists" just come up and get right in people's faces. That is absolutely wrong!

"Who Are You?"

While in Kansas City once, a guy came up to me after a meeting and started railing on my wife. He said, "If you were a man of God, you'd straighten this out. You'd make her do this and that and this other thing." Then he started criticizing and giving me all of his opinions about how my wife should dress. If you knew Jamie, you'd know that my wife is a very conservative dresser. She never wears anything inappropriate. There was nothing wrong with her. This guy just had a bunch of legalistic, religious opinions about jewelry, makeup, and hairstyles that he was trying to force on us.

Basically, I stopped him right in the middle of his tirade, asking, "Who are you?" He told me his name and I said, "No, I mean who gave you the right to speak to us this way? You have no dominion, no right, and no authority over my wife. God did not die and appoint you to take His place. You're nobody. I don't care what your opinion is!"

Of course, this guy was highly offended. His attitude was "How dare you speak to me that way." But since he had the audacity to confront me, rail on my wife, and tell me what to do, I just decided to respond in kind. "Mister, you have no authority in my life."

I would never just walk in and start telling the President of the United States what to do. It's not because I feel inferior. It's not because I don't believe God has given me some valuable things to say. I just recognize that I'd have to earn that right. He would have to request it. I'm not his superior. I can't just force my way in and start spouting opinions.

It's the same for a mail clerk in a business. You may have some ideas that would work, but you can't just barge into the CEO's office and start telling them what to do. You must remain under authority. Now, if they're a good CEO, they'd encourage your feedback. They'd even occasionally go to the hourly workers and ask, "What do you think?" But really, it's his choice to ask for input. You don't have the right—the authority—to just go up to the CEO and start spouting off.

I would never go up to one of the ministers I see on television or hear on the radio and just start rebuking them and telling them things that I disagree with them about. I've listened to some of them, and they are absolutely wrong on some points. God has shown me some truths in His Word that could help them, but I respect them enough to wait to be invited in. I'm not their supervisor. They don't submit to me. We don't have that kind of rapport built up. I'd never do such a thing.

None of Your Business

However, every day someone does that to me. Whether it be in a letter, a phone call, an email, or in person, someone who considers themselves to be the official standard of what's right and wrong reams me up one side and down the other. They've never witnessed to anyone, never seen someone set free, never done anything for the Lord, and yet they think that they know it all.

If they just understood authority, they would stop these kinds of abuses and realize that they have to earn the right to speak into someone's life.

I've told my Bible school students before, "There are some things I know about some of you sitting here right now, problems in your life, however, these problems are outside of school and you haven't come to me about them. If we haven't built a rapport to where I feel like you've opened up to me and given me the freedom to candidly speak to you, then I won't come to you and talk to you about those kinds of things." It's not my place. It's none of my business.

I'll deal with things that affect people while they're at school, but I'm not going to pry into their personal life. Some folks think, *Well, that's wrong. You ought to get more involved.* No, I believe it's wrong for you to stick your nose into other people's business. It really does come down to authority.

Defeated

God is a God of authority. He set structure in place, and He's not going to circumvent it. When one of my employees disagrees with a superior, I tell the person, "Go to your superior and talk to them about it. Don't circumvent the superior by coming to me and trying to get me to counter their opinion." It works better this way. That's how God is. He established authority, and we need to recognize that God Himself obeys it. He would not intervene in the affairs of men until He became a Man. Once He took upon Himself the form of flesh, then He had the authority to take it to the devil. That's good news.

Satan didn't get his authority directly from God. He doesn't have a superior angelic power that he uses over the human race. The devil was stripped of all his angelic power and authority. The power and authority that Satan has used to rule this earth has been mankind's authority that God gave them and they then turned over to Satan.

Understanding that Satan can do nothing in your life without your consent and cooperation puts him down on a plane to where he isn't a superior foe. As a master deceiver, he's still a threat because he can lie to you. You must know the truth and be on guard, but you can resist him.

I know I can win this battle. I can take the power and authority that God has given me, and confront the devil. I'm not ignorant of him, but I'm no longer afraid of him either. I've seen awesome things happen just because I recognize that Satan has been defeated.

Grandma's Room

Like most people who were raised in typical America, I honestly didn't think about demons. I'd read about them in the Bible, but I thought all the demons were overseas in some third world country. I didn't think there were demons here, or that we could physically encounter them. Then I got turned on to the Lord and began to look more closely at the Bible. I recognized that the spirit realm is as real today as it was two thousand years ago. I realized that many different things were demonic, including sicknesses. My friends and I began casting demons out of people and seeing miraculous things happen.

My grandmother raised me until I was about six years old, then she became senile, and eventually died when I was eight. When she died, she left some demons behind in the room she occupied in our house. Right after she passed on, I moved out of the room I was sharing with my brother and into what had been grandmother's room. We had a picture of her sitting on the dresser, and at night it would come alive. Her image would come out of the frame and walk around the room.

Since I was only eight years old, that scared the fire out of me. I knew this was strange, and it wasn't the way it was supposed to be, but I was afraid to tell my mother and father because they would have thought I was crazy. So I just didn't say anything about it, but as soon as possible, I moved out of that room and back in with my brother. He thought, *Well then, I'll take that other room,* and moved in there. It wasn't a month before he moved back in with me. Then my sister took that room. It wasn't a month before she moved back out of there too.

For the next twelve years, we kept that room in our house locked up. Nobody ever said anything, but nobody liked being in there. My older sister brought her newborn daughter home when I was fourteen years old. She'd be sound asleep, but if they walked into that room, she would wake up crying. Then they'd walk out and she'd be okay. Walk in and she'd cry, walk out and she was okay. When I had Bible studies, people would go all over the house to pray with others, but nobody would go in that room. After awhile, my lightning fast mind began to figure out that something was wrong in there.

Not long after I became aware that demons were real and they did exercise influence, I decided to go in that room and cast them out of our house. We always kept the door to that room closed, so I went in and shut the door behind me. I started rebuking and binding and doing everything I could think of. All the hair on the back of my neck stood up. I was afraid and had goose bumps all over me.

In the midst of all this, I remember thinking, *Oh God, I'm so glad I can't see into the spirit realm right now. If I could, I'd see these huge demons towering over me with fangs and claws.* I was envisioning these monstrous demonic powers that were inches away from devouring me, and it was only the name of Jesus that was holding them at bay. I remember praying, "Oh God, thank You that I can't see what's going on in the spirit realm."

Immediately, the Lord spoke to my heart, saying, "Andrew, if I were to show you the spirit realm, instead of seeing these huge powerful demons with fangs and claws, you'd see tiny little imps. You'd be amazed. They're nothing. They just have big mouths. They know how to scream loud and intimidate. They boast of great things, but they can't deliver." As soon as the Lord changed that image from towering demons to tiny little imps who had no power or authority, faith rose up in my heart. Instead of fear, I felt like the Incredible Hulk. A spirit of might and boldness came over me, and I got rid of those demons in no time flat.

You might think, *That was all in your mind.* Well, I didn't tell a single person, but the next time we had a Bible study, people went right into that room without thinking anything about it. There was definitely a difference.

Satan's Only Power

After the devil made all his prideful boasts in Isaiah 14:12–14 saying, "I will do this and I will do that," this passage of scripture goes on to say:

> Yet thou shalt be brought down to hell, to the sides of the pit. They that see thee shall narrowly look upon thee, and consider thee, saying, Is this the man that made the earth to tremble, that did shake kingdoms; that made the world as a wilderness, and destroyed the cities thereof; that opened not the house of his prisoners?
>
> Isaiah 14:15–17

This passage prophesied how people would eventually respond to Satan. Of course, all this has come to pass now that Jesus has literally destroyed the devil through His death, burial, and resurrection. When we see Satan as he really is, we'll say, "Is this the one who intimidated me? Is this the one I allowed to ruin my life? Is this the one I let keep me in bondage—this nothing, this zero?" That's how Satan is. He doesn't have all this power the church has attributed to him. The only power Satan has came from man.

Mankind made Satan. We are the ones who empowered him. God created Lucifer—a ministering spirit, an angelic being. Mankind yielded our God-given dominion, and it's this human authority and power Satan uses. That's why he has to have a body to possess. That's why a pig has more power and authority on this earth than a disembodied demon. Satan is a factor, but only because people yield to him. If you know the truth, the truth will make you free. (John 8:32.) Now that's good news!

CHAPTER 9

Such As I Have

God has given us a huge authority. As born-again believers, Jesus has given us more authority than even Adam and Eve had. They had authority over this earth. However, after Christ rose from the dead, He had authority in heaven, authority on earth, and authority under the earth—meaning the demonic realm and hell. (Phil. 2:10.) After Jesus resurrected, but before He ascended, He turned to His disciples and said:

> All power [authority, power of rule] is given unto me in heaven and in earth. *Go ye therefore,* and teach all nations, baptizing them in the name of the Father, and of the Son, and of the Holy Ghost: teaching them to observe all things whatsoever I have commanded you: and, lo, I am with you alway, even unto the end of the world. Amen.
>
> MATTHEW 28:18–20

Since *therefore* refers to "in light of what I've just said," Jesus was basically telling His followers, "The authority and power I have, I now give to you. Go, and continue doing My work, the work that I have begun."

The authority we have as believers in Christ today is superior to the authority Adam had. We have everything back that he lost, and much more. We now have authority over the demonic realm. (Matt. 10:1,7–8.)

Old vs. New

Compared to the Old Testament, there is a huge difference in the way the New Testament talks about Satan. Although the Old Testament hardly mentions him, the New Testament reveals that Satan is the one who caused different kinds of sicknesses, seizures, convulsions, and blindness. The New Testament reveals many things as being demonic in origin.

Why did God give us this knowledge in the New Testament, but not in the Old? Simply put, even if the Old Testament saints would have known these things, but they couldn't have done anything with this knowledge. It wouldn't have done them any good to know that Satan was behind this or that because they didn't have authority to rebuke the devil or bind him.

Basically, the Old Testament people were told, "Just submit to these laws. With your actions, do these things and don't do these others." By yielding their actions to God in this manner, He was empowered to move in their lives. It also limited what Satan could do. Basically, this was the approach in the Old Testament.

In the New Testament, we now have an authority that has been given to us that enables us to go beyond the surface level. Since we've been given authority over demons, we can go behind the scenes and deal with the demonic powers that are causing sicknesses and diseases and inspiring people to act a certain way. We can see results that Old Testament people could never have seen.

However, along with this superior authority we've been given comes responsibility. This means that since the Lord gave us such power and authority, if we don't use it, then we stop Him from intervening. God flows through us.

God's Power

Jesus gave us power and authority over the devil.

> Then he [Jesus] called his twelve disciples together, and gave them power and authority over all devils, and to cure diseases.
>
> LUKE 9:1

Power here means that we have the ability and the might. We also have the authority to use that ability and might. But with that authority comes responsibility.

> Submit yourselves therefore to God. Resist the devil, and he will flee from you.
>
> JAMES 4:7

That means if we don't resist the devil, he won't flee from us. Although this is very simple, few believers understand it.

Many Christians aren't using the authority that's been given to them. When Satan bothers them—maybe it's through some sickness, disease, poverty, tragedy, or other demonic attack—they approach God as if they don't have any power or authority. They beg God, saying, "Oh Lord, please change this situation. Please get the devil off my back." They don't realize that this isn't within God's authority—He's given that to us.

This is exactly what the Scripture says. We have been given power and authority over all devils." (Luke 9:1.) God gave us authority over the devil. If you're fighting a demonic force, you have the authority to do something about it. Now, you do have to be spiritual enough to discern its origin. Is it truly spiritual, or just something completely natural? If it's truly a demonic attack, then you are responsible to get rid of that demon. You do so using God's power, but that power has been placed under your authority. If you don't use it, it won't be used.

We Must Use It

Many Christians who come to me for counsel and prayer are just powerless. They don't understand that they have any authority. They're begging God to, "Please remove this sickness and prosper me financially. Please save this person." They are begging God to do things that He told them they have the authority to do.

When God said, "You resist the devil, and he will flee from you," that means that if you don't resist the devil, he won't flee. God isn't going to take care of the devil for you. He's already defeated Satan and stripped him of his power. God gave you authority, and if you don't exercise it, He's not going to come and rebuke the devil for you. The battle isn't between God and the devil directly; it's between the devil and us. God has equipped us with authority and power, and we have to use it.

You may wonder, *Well, if it's God's will for us to be healed, then why did this person die?* God gave us the power to heal. It's not our power. It's His power, but it's under our authority. Jesus never told us to pray and ask God to heal people. He told us to go and "heal the sick" (Matt. 10:8).

In the Gospels, Jesus never commanded His disciples to *pray* for the sick, but He did command us to *heal* the sick. (Luke 9:2; 10:9.) The way it's being done in the church today, we basically pray, "Oh Father, we know that You can heal this person. If it's Your will, please—pretty please—do it." We come as beggars, asking. And if we don't see something manifest, if we don't see an instant result, then we wonder, *Why didn't God heal them?* No, God has already released all the healing power it takes for every person on this planet to be healed of every sickness and disease. Jesus took the stripes on His back for our healing, and now He's given us the power to heal the sick. He gave us power and authority over all demons to cast them out and cure diseases. Jesus gave that power to us, and it's up to us to use it.

Walking, Leaping, and Praising God

Consider Peter and John at the temple gate.

> Now Peter and John went up together into the temple at the hour of prayer, being the ninth hour. And a certain man lame from his mother's womb was carried, whom they laid daily at the gate of the temple which is called Beautiful, to ask alms of them that entered into the temple; who seeing Peter and John about to go into the temple asked an alms. And Peter, fastening his eyes upon him with John, said, Look on us. And he gave heed unto them, expecting to receive something of them.
>
> Then Peter said, Silver and gold have I none; but such as *I have* give I thee: In the name of Jesus Christ of Nazareth rise up and walk. And he took him by the right hand, and lifted him up: and immediately his feet and ankle bones received strength. And he leaping up stood, and walked, and entered with them into the temple, walking, and leaping, and praising God.
>
> ACTS 3:1–8

Notice in verse 6 that Peter said, "Such as I have, give I unto you" (author paraphrase). Peter and John would be kicked out of most churches around the world today for saying, "I have the power to heal you." It's become fashionable for us to say, "Oh, it's not me. I couldn't heal a gnat." Well, the truth is none of us can heal a gnat in our own human power. But we aren't only human, we're born again! God gave us power and authority—the right and ability to use that power. So Peter was absolutely correct when he said, "Such as I have, give I unto you."

Notice in this instance that Peter never even prayed a prayer. Most people would think that was terrible. *How dare him heal someone without praying and asking God!* I don't know about you, but I'm after results—and Peter got the right results. His approach to this situation is the proper approach. Peter said, "Such as I have, give I unto you." Peter knew he had power. He knew he had the authority to use that power. So he took responsibility and used that power. Because of it, that man was healed.

This is the very reason many people aren't seeing healing today. They're coming to God and begging Him. They don't understand that the power doesn't reside in heaven. God has placed the power to heal on the inside of every born-again believer. He's also given us the authority to use it, which makes us responsible. If someone isn't healed, it's not God who didn't heal them—it's us not using our authority and power.

It's Our Turn

Of course, there may be some other dynamics involved. It's not always the individual's fault receiving the prayer. It could be the fault of the other people around them. Jesus operated in absolute faith, but He had to put out scoffers and unbelievers. Christ operated in faith perfectly, yet...

> He could there [in His hometown] do no mighty work...because of their unbelief.
>
> MARK 6:5,6

The limit wasn't in Him, but in the people around Him. The limit isn't always in the person receiving the healing. There could be other factors round about. However, it always comes back to some person or group of people who are limiting God because they aren't taking the authority God has given and exercising it. We are shirking our responsibility, and we're trying to put all the responsibility off on God, saying it's His fault whether or not this person gets saved, healed, or prospered. That's absolutely wrong.

We need to understand and recognize that it's not God's turn to heal. It's our turn to believe that He's already healed. We must accept that power, take that authority, and use it. We need to speak to our problems and command things to change.

If we could get this truth down, it would make a huge difference in the way things happen today. The vast majority of the body of Christ believes that God can do whatever He wants, but they don't believe that He's already done it. They don't believe that He's given us power. So, they don't feel any responsibility to take and use their authority. This is where the system is breaking down. God has already done His part. He's placed the power and authority on the inside of us, which makes us responsible.

For additional information about what God has already done and what He's placed inside of you as a born-again believer, I recommend *Spirit, Soul & Body*, and *You've Already Got It!* These two teachings of mine are foundational, and will really help you receive and experience God's best.

We Were Healed

Through the death, burial, and resurrection of the Lord Jesus Christ, God has already done His part. Now it is up to you to respond in faith and receive His provision. It's totally your responsibility to get healed, prospered, and delivered. It's God's power, but He's placed it under your authority.

Although I'm strongly emphasizing our responsibility, there's no need to come under any condemnation. (Rom. 8:1.) The Lord loves you and wants you to understand these truths so you can enjoy the abundant life He's provided. That's why it's so important to understand our responsibility.

You may be asking, "So do I have to make all this happen?" Not out of your self—your human ability. The born-again part of you—your spirit—has God's power within. All things are possible to those who believe. (Mark 9:23.) If you would understand and believe that God has already done His part, and then exercise your authority, you could make things happen.

Since I've understood and applied these truths, I've seen a huge improvement in my life and ministry. I've prayed for people to be healed for many years. In the beginning, I'd see someone healed every once in awhile, but I didn't have a clue what I was doing. Even an old blind squirrel will come up with a nut every once in awhile if he just keeps trying. I just prayed for so many people that every once in awhile something would happen and we'd see healing manifest. Since then, I've come to realize that it's not me petitioning and asking the Lord to heal people, but rather that God has already healed us of all sickness and disease.

The Word says that by His stripes we *were*—past tense—healed. (1 Pet. 2:24.) Now I understand that God has put His power in me, and it's up to me to release it. God has done His part, now I must take my authority, speak to the mountain, and command people to be healed. Of course, the individual I'm ministering to must believe and cooperate too, but I've seen hundreds of times more people healed than I used to.

John G. Lake

John G. Lake had a healing ministry back in the early 1900s. He was so effective in ministering healing that the state of Washington actually gave him a medical license. He opened up a hospital in Spokane where he lived, and saw so many documented cases of people being healed that they literally closed one of the other hospitals in town.

In Lake's hospital, they didn't administer medicine. They just came around with the Word, anointed patients with oil, and prayed with them until they saw the healing manifest. He trained others how to minister healing and called them "practitioners." For cases that couldn't come to the hospital, Lake sent out his practitioners to make house calls. Based on James 5:14–15, he'd give them a little bottle of oil and tell them, "Don't come back until they're healed."

This kind of boldness just startles people today. They think, *How could you do that? You don't have any control over this. You don't have that kind of authority. You don't have any responsibility. Just go out and ask God to heal them. He might, He might not. Whatever will be, will be. It's all up to God, you see.* Not true.

John G. Lake and his practitioners knew that God had already done His part to provide healing and that it's our turn now to take our authority and use it. The longest time any of those practitioners stayed out ministering was about thirty days. Sometimes they would literally move in with the people and teach them the Word. They'd build them up in faith, minister to them, and see them healed because God has already done His part.

There's a huge difference between us healing the sick and praying for the sick. As a whole, the church has believed God can heal, but not that He has already done it. They don't believe that He has already committed the power and authority for healing to us. So when they have a need, they approach God like a beggar. They ask Him to heal so-and-so when the truth is that He's already done His part to produce that healing. God has placed supernatural raising-from-the-dead power on the inside of every born-again believer (Eph. 1:19–20), and it's up to us to command those healings to come to pass. Instead of passively pleading with the Lord and asking God to do it, we need to become a commander—someone who stands up in faith, takes our authority in Christ, and commands the power of God.

CHAPTER 10

Command Ye Me

To heal the lame man, Peter stood in faith, took his authority in Christ, and commanded the power of God. (Acts 3:6-8.) A lot of people say, "Well, I'd never do that," which is why they aren't getting the results that Peter and John did. This is one of the major reasons we aren't seeing the power of God manifest more today.

Many Christians are in need of a miracle. It's critical. Maybe you need healing in your body, a financial provision, or restoration in your marriage. Whatever it is, you are praying and asking God but you aren't taking any authority over the enemy, you aren't speaking against the problem, and you aren't commanding the infirmity to leave. You're acting like a beggar instead of the commander Christ has authorized and empowered you to be.

Old Sinner or Saved By Grace?

Religion says, "You can't do anything. You're a worm. You are nothing." That's true if you're talking about my carnal, natural, fleshly self. Jesus said:

> Without me ye can do nothing.
>
> JOHN 15:5

That is absolutely true. Apart from Christ, we are and can do nothing. However, I am not without Jesus. I'm born again. The Spirit of the Living God dwells on the inside of me. I'm not only human. Jesus Himself lives in and through me. (Gal. 2:20.)

Christians who don't recognize that, in Christ, they've become a brand-new creation aren't taking their God-given authority. They don't understand the authority of the believer. They come to God as beggars, saying, "I'm an old sinner saved by grace."

I'm not an old sinner saved by grace. I was an old sinner, but then I was saved by grace. Now I've become the righteousness of God in Christ Jesus. (2 Cor. 5:21.) It's true that without God I'm nothing, but I'm not without God. He lives on the inside of me. Now I have the authority and power to command the power of God.

Under Your Command

Keep in mind that this authority that Jesus has given us only enforces spiritual law. If God hasn't provided something, then we can't just command it. Taking and using the authority Jesus has given isn't us "making" God do things.

> Thus saith the LORD, the Holy One of Israel, and his Maker, Ask me of things to come concerning my sons, and *concerning the work of my hands command ye me.*
>
> ISAIAH 45:11

The last part of this verse is a strong statement that many people choke on. They can't receive it because they think to do so would be to take authority over God and tell Him, "Lord, You obey me. I command You to do this." Certainly, that's ridiculous.

I am not God. I'm not superior to Him. It's not me that is the power source. God isn't waiting on my every whim, and obeying what I tell Him to do. That's not what Isaiah 45:11 is talking about. The Lord said, concerning the work of My hands, you command Me. This means that God has told me to command the work of His hands—which is everything He's already provided in Christ—into manifestation.

It's like electricity. The power company is the source—they generate the power. You aren't the power source. You could stick a light bulb in your mouth, but it'll never come on. The power company generates the power and delivers it to your home. You've signed a contract, and that power is under your command.

If you want the power to come on, you don't call the power company and ask them to come out and turn it on. No. They've already generated that power and delivered it to you. Now it's up to you to command that power. When you go over and flip that switch, you are commanding that power. You aren't the source, but the power is under your control. It's under your authority. So you use that authority and switch it on.

Flip the Switch

Now, if the power company doesn't generate the electricity, you could flip that switch all you want, but if there's no power there, nothing is going to happen.

If someone who wasn't yet born again tried to speak to sickness or a demon and command them to leave, it wouldn't work. Nothing would happen because they don't have the power of God inside them. This is what happened to the seven sons of Sceva (see Acts 19:11–16). These lost men saw Paul expelling demons in the name of Jesus, and tried to do the same. But the demons inside the man they were trying to deliver rose up and caused the man to beat up those seven lost men and send them away bleeding. If you aren't connected to the power source, if you aren't truly born again, you can't do what I'm sharing with you. But if you are truly born again and have received the power of the Holy Spirit according to Acts 1:8, then that power is in you, and it's up to you to command it.

If you called the power company and said, "I have some friends coming over for lunch. Would you please turn on the power? I need it to cook the food, have light, and play soft music." It doesn't matter how much you plead or how serious your need is, the power company isn't going to send somebody out to flip the switch for you. They generate the power, but you must take your position of authority and flip the switch.

Many Christians today are praying and asking God to come over and flip their switch. They don't realize that He's placed that power on the inside of them. They don't recognize their responsibility to flip their own switch. They aren't believing God's Word which reveals that they now have the power, authority, and responsibility to go and heal the sick. Instead of commanding and releasing this power that's been given to them, they pray and ask God to heal the sick. That's just as silly as asking the electric company to come over and turn on your lights!

"The Donkey I Ride On"

One of the first times a friend of mine went to Africa to minister, God dealt with him on this very issue. At his meetings, he saw all kinds of great miracles, including many people healed. As a result of this, the African people were just overwhelmed. As my friend walked through the city streets, people would run up to him screaming, yelling, and wanting to touch him. His first reaction was, "It's not me. It's God. Don't look to me!" But before he could say anything, the Lord spoke to his heart, saying, "When I rode into

Jerusalem, all the people were throwing palm branches and garments down in My path, singing 'Hosanna—glory to God in the highest!' What would you have thought if that donkey I was riding on would have said, 'Oh, it's not me. It's not me'?" The Lord continued, saying, "It's not you that they are yelling about and trying to touch—it's Me. You're just the donkey that I ride on." Once my friend saw that, he started walking around and letting people touch him.

Some people take offense at this and say, "You just think you're somebody special!" No, I'm nobody special. There is nothing special in me, but I carry the most special Person who has ever walked the face of this earth. The Lord Jesus Christ lives on the inside of me, and He's given me His power and anointing. Just like Peter's shadow touched people and they were healed, I'm believing for a day when my shadow will do the same. I'm believing they will lay the sick in the streets and my shadow will fall upon them and heal them. Some people might think, *Well, you arrogant thing!* It's not me, it's Who I carry. He's the same Person Peter carried. If it worked for him, it'll work for me.

Scores of Christians are so focused on the physical, carnal, natural side of who they are that they don't recognize that they aren't only human. They don't realize that they've been given supernatural power and authority. That's why they aren't seeing the power of God.

There is a religious culture today that is against everything I'm teaching. It comes against this authority and tries to make you feel like you're nothing, that you have no power and no authority. You come to God as a beggar, pleading with Him to do what He's told you in His Word that He's already done. He told you to go out and represent Him so stop begging and pleading, bawling and squalling, and asking God to do things that it's not His turn to do. Take a stand, use your authority, and command things to come to pass.

Joe Blow Believer

Jesus commissioned His disciples and sent them out saying:

> Heal the sick, cleanse the lepers, raise the dead, cast out devils: freely ye have received, freely give.
>
> MATTHEW 10:8

You can't give away something you don't have. If you don't believe that God has already done His part and put that raising-from-the-dead power on the inside of you, then you can't go out and heal the sick, cleanse the lepers, or raise the dead. I wish I could just make people believe these truths, but I know I'm fighting against hundreds of years of religious traditions that have made the Word of God of none effect. (Mark 7:13.) God has already healed every person that will ever be healed. That power has already been generated and is now deposited on the inside of every born-again, Spirit-filled, tongue-talking believer. You have that power. It's not up to God to heal the sick. It's up to us to believe, take our authority, release that power, and command these things to happen. We must give—minister—this healing power to other people.

I really enjoy watching our Charis Bible College students and alumni minister at our citywide meetings—Gospel Truth Seminars. In the past, when I ministered in churches, after I built up the people's faith with the Word, I'd stay there praying with them for hours. The people would come to me by the hundreds and I would pray for them and see blind eyes and deaf ears open and other miracles and healings. After three or four hours of that, I was excited, but I was also worn-out. I knew I was limited. I'd see all the people lined up for prayer and know that I wouldn't be able to make it to the end of the line. People couldn't wait that long, so they'd leave because I just couldn't minister to them.

Then we started going into larger venues and instead of having two or three hundred people, we started having five hundred or a thousand people come to my meetings. There was just no way that I could minister to all of them, so the Lord told me to teach these truths to our Bible College students—these truths that you have the power on the inside of you and you can command healings to come to pass. Now I have students and alumni help me minister in these larger meetings. Instead of only me being able to pray for a hundred or so people, together we're praying for five hundred people or more per night. We're seeing blind eyes and deaf ears open, people come out of wheelchairs, and all kinds of miracles. I'm thrilled to know that it isn't just a supernatural gift flowing through one individual that everything has to funnel through. This is for Joe Blow Believer!

Minister His Power to Others

One of our prayer ministers had never prayed for another person and seen a physical miracle happen in his life. The very first night he began to pray with people, he ministered to a blind man who received his sight. This fellow who had never witnessed a physical miracle in all his life was so excited that he didn't sleep all night. He came back the next day telling everyone on the team all about it.

I'm not against people who have a supernatural gift. There is a place for that in the body of Christ. But some folks have thought that they have to be one of these healing evangelist miracle ministries in order to be able to pray for people. As this prayer minister found out, that's not so. Every born-again, Spirit-filled believer has been given power and authority to heal the sick, cleanse the leper, and raise the dead. (Matt. 10:8.) The Lord has commanded us to give—minister—that power to other people.

CHAPTER 11

Proclaim and Demonstrate

> Whatsoever city ye enter...heal the sick that are therein, and say unto them, The kingdom of God is come nigh unto you.
>
> LUKE 10:8,9

Jesus told us to heal the sick *and* preach the kingdom of God. However, so much of the church has just chosen to ignore the first part of our commission. Proclamation and demonstration should always go hand in hand. God's Word needs to be confirmed with signs, wonders, and miracles.

The Spirit-filled side of the church desires to see miracles and healings, but the way so many of them are going about it is to beg and plead with God, saying, "Oh God, I ask You to pour out Your Spirit. Do a new thing, and send revival." That's not the approach the people in the Bible took. They believed that God had given them the authority. They went out and brought revival, commanded revival, and released revival by seeing miracles happen.

More Than Just Doctrine

Consider the disciples who had been arrested and commanded not to preach the Gospel anymore.

> Being let go, they went to their own company, and reported all that the chief priests and elders had said unto them. And when they heard that, they lifted up their voice to God with one accord, and said, Lord...behold their threatenings: and grant unto thy servants, that with all boldness they may speak thy word, by stretching forth thine hand to heal; and that signs and wonders may be done by the name of thy holy child Jesus.
>
> ACTS 4:23,24,29,30

Notice how they prayed. "God, help us to preach Your Word." How? "By stretching forth Your hand to heal" (author paraphrase). This is the way that the early New Testament church preached the Gospel. It wasn't just doctrine. There was both proclamation and demonstration in the power of the Spirit. They prayed, "Lord, help us to preach Your Word by healing the sick *and* seeing Your power manifest." That's how they went out to minister, and that's the reason they saw better results than most folks are getting today.

There ought to be a difference between how you preach and how false religions preach. They don't accept Jesus as the only begotten Son of God, the only way to the Father. Yet, when many Christians go out and knock on a door, they are no different than the followers of false religions who go door to door to get new converts. All they have is a doctrine. Proper doctrine is important, but it's not the only thing that should separate a true believer in Christ from those who aren't.

A true Christian is a person who not only has a proper doctrine about who Jesus is, but they can also demonstrate it by the power and gifts of the Holy Spirit. Why isn't this happening more? The reason is that we are praying and asking God to do what He commanded us to do.

Command Healing to Manifest

The Lord told us to go heal the sick. He didn't tell us to pray and ask Him to heal the sick. Jesus told us to do it. God is the power source, but He's placed that power on the inside of us. He gave us the authority to use His name and His power. If we don't command healing to come, it won't happen. It's not going to come by us begging and asking God to heal.

Perhaps you know someone who has an incurable disease. You've been praying and asking God to heal them. You've been trying to lay hold of God for healing, and you haven't seen the manifestation yet. You're fighting fear, doubt, and frustration. You need to recognize that you're asking God to do what He asked you to do. God told you to go heal the sick. He told you to give—minister—His healing power. Just like Peter and John, you need to take your authority and command healing to manifest.

Cecil Paxton trains people how to receive and minister healing. He used to oversee our ministry Helpline, but now travels widely preaching, teaching, and ministering all around the world. Back when he lived in Colorado Springs, a mutual friend of ours had a stroke and went blind. Cecil went over to this man's house and ministered to him. Cecil took his authority and commanded those eyes to open. In an instant, those totally blind eyes opened and the man could see perfectly. Cecil took his authority in Christ, commanded the healing to manifest, and it did.

Cecil's wife, Lisa, has a powerful testimony of God's healing power. It's available in audio as "Lisa Paxton's Testimony" or in booklet form as *Lisa's Story*. You'll be encouraged!

God's Will

God desires for every person to respond to Him and receive salvation.

> The Lord is not slack concerning his promise, as some men count slackness; but is longsuffering to us-ward, not willing that any should perish, but that all should come to repentance.
>
> 2 PETER 3:9

God doesn't will for a single person to die and go to hell. Does that mean everyone will receive salvation? No, obviously not. Jesus said:

> Enter ye in at the strait gate: for wide is the gate, and broad is the way, that leadeth to destruction, and many there be which go in thereat: because strait is the gate, and narrow is the way, which leadeth unto life, and few there be that find it.
>
> MATTHEW 7:13,14

The Bible clearly reveals that God's will doesn't just automatically come to pass.

So much religion and tradition in the church today misrepresents God. It says, "Nothing happens without His direct or indirect approval. God either causes it or allows it." This is not what the Word teaches. The reason this doctrine is so popular and people latch onto it is that it gives them an excuse and frees them from all personal responsibility. In other words, you can just pray, "Lord, if it's Your will, please heal this person. If it's Your will, save this marriage." Then if it works—great. If it doesn't, then it must not have been God's will. This thinking takes us totally out of the picture. We have no responsibility or accountability in the matter. This is absolutely wrong!

People Have a Choice

Second Peter 3:9 clearly reveals that it's not God's will that anyone perish. Yet, people are perishing—lots of them. God doesn't control or just allow these things. He's not the One who "predestined" some people to be saved and others to be lost. There are a number of reasons why people are perishing instead of being saved.

Each individual person has a choice. God isn't going to force anyone to be saved. He honors our free will. Some people—due to the lies and deception of the devil, or because they've been hurt and taken up an offense—are preoccupied with the cares of this life. They have rejected all of the invitations and interventions of God in their life. So, by their own free will, they are choosing not to make Jesus their Lord. Your faith can't make a person get saved. That's not what the Word of God teaches.

> Believe on the Lord Jesus Christ, and thou shalt be saved, and thy house.
>
> ACTS 16:31

In context, this is saying, "Believe on the Lord Jesus Christ and you will be saved. And as each one of your family members believe on Him, they'll be saved too."

Each person must believe on the Lord Jesus Christ and receive salvation for themselves. No one can do it for you, and you can't do it for someone else. People have a choice in the matter.

Misrepresenting the Lord

Sometimes the problem is that we're misrepresenting the Gospel, the Lord, and His kingdom. We aren't telling people the truth. We're giving them religion and tradition or our words aren't matching our life.

For whatever reason, many people are led into false religions. Some are being told that to kill people for religious purposes grants them entrance into heaven with a harem of women throughout all eternity. That is absolute foolishness. It's completely wrong, and violates the truth of God's Word. Yet, there are people full of misplaced hope and zeal engaged in suicide bombings and other similar activities. False doctrines are sending lots of people to hell.

If God doesn't desire any of this, then why is it happening? God gave us authority and with it comes responsibility. In order to see people born again, we must preach the Gospel. It's not because God hasn't done everything necessary to provide salvation that people aren't born again. It's not because He doesn't want them saved. One major reason people aren't being born again is that Christians haven't taken their authority and used it properly.

Perhaps believers aren't preaching the true Gospel. They're ministering religion and tradition instead. Maybe some Christians presented a negative witness with their lifestyle. Perhaps the lost person had one bad experience with someone who said they were a believer, and because of it refuses to really listen to the true claims of Christ. Some way or another, it's people who are messing things up. Satan is inspiring it. He's doing his best to prejudice people against the Gospel. It's not God's will that any person die and go to hell, yet it's happening.

This same logic applies to healing, prosperity, and marriages. People say, "Well, if it's God's will, they'll be healed whether you or I pray for them or not." Apply the same reasoning to salvation and see how it sounds. "If it's God's will, people will be saved whether we minister to them or not." That's not true. We have a responsibility. We've been given power and authority to preach the Gospel.

Preach the Gospel

That's what I'm doing. I'm sharing the Word of God with as many people as I can. There are millions of folks being touched by our daily television, radio, and Internet ministry. People are hearing the Word of God and their lives are being changed. They're being born again, baptized in the Holy Spirit, healed, delivered, and set free. It's always been God's will to set them free, but they hadn't heard the truth. Somebody had to come across their path and share it with them.

> How then shall they call on him in whom they have not believed? and how shall they believe in him of whom they have not heard? and how shall they hear without a preacher? And how shall they preach, except they be sent...So then faith cometh by hearing, and hearing by the word of God.
>
> Romans 10:14,15,17

It's not God's will for anyone to perish, but God relies on people to minister His Word and cause different things to change. God has given us both the authority and the responsibility to preach the Gospel. If we don't take that responsibility and use that authority, the Word won't be preached and people won't get saved. It's not God's will for our nation or this world to be in the mess it's in. His will is for us all to reflect His values, submit to Him, and shine as a glorious church. However, it's not working that way because people aren't responding to Him properly.

Let's stop begging God to do what He has told us to do. Instead of asking Him to send revival and save people, we need to go out and preach the Gospel with signs and wonders. Let's take what Jesus has already provided and make it manifest. It's His power, but it's our authority (which He gave us) that makes it work. God's power is released as we use our authority. Go ahead, flip the switch!

CHAPTER 12

Be a Witness

> When they therefore were come together, they asked of him, saying, Lord, wilt thou at this time restore again the kingdom to Israel? And he said unto them, It is not for you to know the times or the seasons, which the Father hath put in his own power.
>
> Acts 1:6,7

I remember a guy who wrote a book proposing eighty-eight reasons why the Lord would return in 1988. I talked with some people who honestly believed what he said was true. With all of their heart, they were counting on the Lord coming back in 1988. Of course, it didn't happen. So then he wrote a book detailing eighty-nine reasons why the Lord would return in 1989—and people bought that book too. The guy totally missed it, yet a bunch of folks still came out and swallowed the very next thing he had to say. How dumb can you get and still breathe?

Acts 1:6–7 is saying that you can't know the time or the season that Jesus is coming back to fully establish His kingdom. If someone tells you that they know and they're predicting some date, then you can just write "Ichabod" across their forehead (that's Old Testament terminology for "the glory has departed";[1] 1 Sam. 4:21). I guarantee you they are in deception, and it's not God.

Immediately after the Lord said, "You don't have power or authority concerning those kinds of things because the Father has reserved them for Himself," He continued saying:

> But ye shall receive power, after that the Holy Ghost is come upon you: and ye shall be witnesses unto me both in Jerusalem, and in all Judaea, and in Samaria, and unto the uttermost part of the earth.
>
> ACTS 1:8

Jesus told His disciples, *you* will have power to be a witness. Think about it. The Lord would never give you a position without also giving you the authority to execute and accomplish what He told you to do. So with this power to be a witness comes an authority to be a witness—and all the responsibility that goes along with it.

Through People

Peter exercised this power and authority to be a witness when he followed God's leading to Cornelius' house.

> There was a certain man in Caesarea called Cornelius, a centurion of the band called the Italian band, a devout man, and one that feared God with all his house, which gave much alms to the people, and prayed to God always. He saw in a vision evidently about the ninth hour of the day an angel of God coming in to him, and saying unto him, Cornelius. And when he looked on him, he was afraid, and said, What is it, Lord? And he said unto him, Thy prayers and thine alms are come up for a memorial before God. And now send men to Joppa, and call for one Simon, whose surname is Peter. He lodgeth with one Simon a tanner, whose house is by the sea side: he shall tell thee what thou oughtest to do.
>
> ACTS 10:1–6

An angel appeared to this centurion and said, "Cornelius, you're a devout man. God has heard your prayers. Now send to Joppa and ask for Peter. He'll come and tell you how to be born again." Why didn't this angel tell Cornelius the Gospel? It would have been much more efficient than sending men on a two day journey (one way) to bring Peter back. Why didn't this angel just tell him how to be born again? The answer is simple: God gave power and authority to people to preach the Gospel, not to angels. Angels don't have the authority to preach the Gospel—we do. God has limited Himself to preaching the Gospel through people.

God's plan is for us to preach the truth of the Gospel, and for people to hear it and be born again through the incorruptible seed of God's Word. However, Satan has come in through religious teaching, saying, "You don't have to share God's Word. Just *pray* them into the kingdom." So now there are all these Christians who are praying and asking God to save people, and they never share the Gospel with them.

I've actually met people before who say they are "prayer warriors" who never get out of their closet. Their prayer list is so long, they can't even read it all in an hour. They diligently work through their list and pray for everybody, but they won't witness to a neighbor. They don't talk to people at the grocery store. They won't speak to their mailman. They don't share the Word with anyone, but they're praying for a "great move of God." That's deception. It doesn't happen that way. You can't pray a person into the kingdom of God.

Faith Comes by Hearing

You have to be born again by the incorruptible seed of God's Word.

> Being born again, not of corruptible seed, but of incorruptible, by the word of God, which liveth and abideth for ever.
>
> 1 PETER 1:23

God's Word is the seed. It must be planted in the ground of our heart. This is also like sowing a seed in the womb of a woman. You can't conceive a child apart from this seed being sown. There was only one virgin birth, and there isn't going to be another. You must get out of your prayer closet and sow the seed of God's Word.

> Faith cometh by hearing, and hearing by the word of God.
>
> ROMANS 10:17

You can't be born again without faith, and that faith comes through the seed of God's Word.

Plant the Seed

You don't get pregnant through prayer. You can receive healing through prayer, which may affect your ability to get pregnant, but you don't get pregnant through just prayer. I've prayed with many couples who were unable to have children who later went on to conceive supernaturally, but my prayer wasn't what made them pregnant.

One time a woman came forward and asked me to pray that she'd get pregnant. Right before I put my hands on her, I felt impressed to ask, "Are you married?" She answered, "No, I'm not." I pulled my hands back really quick. I wasn't going to have anything to do with this lady getting pregnant if she wasn't married. That's not God's will. Prayer doesn't make you pregnant. You have to plant that seed.

Many Christians are praying for people to be born again, but they're not praying about the planting of the seed. They're not praying for someone to come across their path and preach the Gospel to these people. (Matt. 9:38.) They aren't asking the Holy Spirit to bring back to their memory the words God has already spoken to them. (John 14:26.) They're just thinking that they can pray somebody into the kingdom. That violates the power and authority God gave us when He told us to go preach the Gospel. The angel didn't tell Cornelius how to get saved; Peter—a physical human being—had to do that. You need to understand that God gave the power, authority, and responsibility for preaching the Gospel to people.

You may have been praying for someone for many years, but you're frustrated and wondering, *Why isn't God saving this person?* It may be because you aren't praying right. Are you asking God to save them as if there were something He could do? He's already done His part to provide salvation through the death, burial, and resurrection of Jesus Christ. The Lord commissioned us to preach the Gospel. If that person hasn't received salvation, it's either because they aren't hearing the true Gospel, or they're choosing to reject it. It's not God who isn't saving that individual. There are ways you can pray to speed things up and enable the Holy Spirit to minister to this person more, but just praying and asking God, "Please save them" is useless. That's not how the Word teaches us to do it.

The Truth

You may be tempted to be offended right now, feeling like I'm saying that God is limited in power. No, I'm saying that God has limited Himself by His own Word. He told us to preach the Gospel. He said that people are born again by the incorruptible seed of God's Word. If we don't follow His instructions, then we can't expect the proper results.

Perhaps you choose to say, "God, I'm not going to talk to them. I don't want to get out there and risk suffering any embarrassment, shame, or persecution that might come by me speaking the Word. I'm just going to pray in my closet and believe that You're going to do a miracle." If this is you, then you're just spitting in the wind. It isn't going to work because that's not how the kingdom operates.

I'm speaking this truth in love. If we ask God to save someone, but we don't do what He commanded us to do—which is preach the Gospel and be a witness—then it isn't going to happen. People must be born again through the Word of God. Prayer doesn't cause people to be born again. Prayer may help once you've already shared the Gospel, but it's not a substitute for doing what God has told us to do. People don't get born again just through prayer; they get born again through hearing the truth.

> Ye shall know the truth, and the truth shall make you free.
>
> JOHN 8:32

The devil has deceived people into just praying and asking God to do what He has commanded us to do. He's commanded us to preach the Gospel. Cornelius had an angel appear to him in response to his prayers, but the angel didn't preach the Gospel to him. Instead, he told him to send men to Joppa to bring Peter back to tell them how to be born again. Angels don't have the authority to preach the Gospel. God didn't commit that to them. It's our responsibility.

God Loves People

I pray. I spend a lot of time just fellowshipping and communing with the Lord. The vast majority of my prayer life is worshiping God, thanking the Lord, and asking Him for wisdom and instruction. As far as my ministry to others, I ask God to help me speak His Word with clarity and boldness. I pray that He would give me revelation knowledge, and better ways of communicating it to others.

However, I don't spend any time asking God to "move" and save people. I don't pray, "Oh, Lord. Please touch their hearts and cause them to be born again." That's because I know that God loves them more than I do. I'm convinced that He wants to touch their lives and see them born again. I don't plead with Him, saying, "Please love these people and move in their lives." Since God is love, He's led me to do everything I can—including broadcasting daily programs on television and radio around the world, giving away lots of free materials at my Web site, translating my books into multiple languages, and starting new branches of Charis Bible College all the time—to share the truth of God's Word with as many people as possible. The Lord knows that as people receive the truth into their heart, it will make them free.

Since I know that God already loves people and wants to minister to them, I don't spend any time pleading with Him to love, touch, and move in these people's lives. I'm aware that what I am sharing is very different from the way many folks pray. Yet, most people aren't getting very good results from their prayer life. If that's you, maybe you ought to try something different. What I'm telling you about works.

In my teaching *A Better Way to Pray,* I cover this topic of prayer much more comprehensively. If you'd like the results of your prayer life to improve, I strongly encourage you to check it out.

Politics and Prayer

When I first started in the ministry, I used to plead with God for an outpouring of His Spirit. I started all night prayer meetings where we just cried, wailed, and travailed, begging God to send revival. I had divided the city where I lived—Arlington, Texas—up into sections, and was praying over each one of them, saying, "Oh God, please touch these people. Oh Lord, we've got to have a move!" I gave Him all of the statistics in order to impress on Him how important this was, telling Him, "You've got to do something!" I was trying to manipulate, motivate, and twist God's arm.

Finally, as I beat my fist against the wall for emphasis, these words came flying out of my mouth: "God, if You loved the people of Arlington, Texas, half as much as I do, we'd have revival!" As soon as those words left my mouth, I immediately thought, *Something is wrong with this prayer. Here I am presenting to God that I love these people and want to see them ministered to more than He does.* My lightning fast mind figured out that I was making some serious mistakes.

The truth is, much of the church is still doing this. They're begging, "Oh God, send revival. Oh Lord, if You wanted to, You could pour out Your Spirit on our country and things would change." That's not true. God moves on this earth through His people. (Eph. 3:20.) He moves as we preach, teach, and act on His Word. He moves through us as we obey the promptings of the Holy Spirit. Satan is the one behind some of these "movements" in the body of Christ today that are getting us into doing everything except preaching the Gospel.

Although it's important for Christians to exercise their civic duty and vote, it's a deception of the devil to put all of our faith, energy, effort, and hope into the political process. Political action has its place in a believer's life, but it's not the primary avenue through which the church should influence a nation. The political process is not the strength of the church—the Gospel is.

The founding fathers of the United States—many of whom were active Christians—said that democracy is totally unsuited for anyone but a moral people. John Adams (our first vice-president and second president) said that if we ever cease to be moral, democracy will destroy this nation. That's literally what we see happening today.

We're legalizing immorality, changing the Constitution, and ignoring the clear intent of our founding fathers.

The Strength of the Church

The real strength of the church is in preaching the Gospel. As God's Word changes the hearts of men and women, the political arena will reflect it. The reason so many laws promoting immorality are being proposed right now is the church hasn't been doing its job. We haven't been preaching the truth. We've lost the hearts of people, and those hearts are now using the political process to pass laws favoring their preferences toward sin. The church would do much more to change our nation by preaching the Gospel and teaching God's Word than by immersing ourselves completely into the political process or by locking ourselves in the prayer closet for hours on end begging and pleading with God for revival.

The Lord told us to go out and preach the Gospel. As people receive the truth into their hearts, the truth will set them free. That's where our strength lies. God told us to influence our nation by ministering His Word because the number one power of the church is the proclamation and demonstration of the Gospel. (Rom. 1:16.)

Instead of boldly sharing God's truth, many Christians have retreated to their prayer closets. They're afraid to say anything in front of people lest somebody deem them "politically incorrect." So they run to the prayer closet, begging God for revival and pleading with Him to do what He's told us to do.

> It pleased God by the foolishness of preaching [the Gospel] to save them that believe.
>
> 1 Corinthians 1:21

You can't be born again without hearing the Word of God. As believers today, let's properly emphasize His Word. Let's boldly share the truth with everyone we can. Let's not use politics or ineffective "prayer" to shirk our responsibility to preach the Gospel, but let's be faithful, consistent, and powerful witnesses of our Lord Jesus Christ.

CHAPTER 13

How to Pray for the Lost

I'd like to share with you some biblical ways to effectively pray for a lost person. This kind of prayer is like water. Once the seed of God's Word is planted, it must be watered. Prayer isn't a substitute for planting a seed. You can water barren ground all you like, but it won't produce a harvest. You must plant the seed of God's Word for people to be born again. However, these are some good ways to pray and water the seed that's been planted.

As you start praying for a lost person, you need to recognize that God loves them infinitely more than you do.

> God so loved the world, that he gave his only begotten Son, that whosoever believeth in him should not perish, but have everlasting life.
>
> JOHN 3:16

The Lord doesn't want any lost person to perish, but to repent, turn to Him, and enjoy everlasting life.

> The Lord is not slack concerning his promise, as some men count slackness; but is longsuffering to us-ward, not willing that any should perish, but that all should come to repentance.
>
> 2 PETER 3:9

In light of these truths, you could start praying for a lost individual by thanking God, saying, "Father, I thank You that You love this person so much that You gave Your only begotten Son for them. It's not Your will for them to perish, but to come to repentance and turn to You. I thank You, Lord, that You've already provided for their salvation."

> [Jesus] is the propitiation for our sins: and not for ours only, but also for the sins of the whole world.
>
> 1 JOHN 2:2

God not only loves the whole world, but He's already died for the sins of the whole world. He's already paid for them. A person who goes to hell is going there with their sins paid for. The reason they go to hell is that they reject the payment—they refuse to believe and receive the Lord Jesus Christ.

Laborers Across Their Path

You can continue praying, "Father, I thank You that You've already made provision. Jesus, You were the atoning sacrifice for everyone's sins—not only those who believe, but also those who are lost. So, Father, I thank You that You want them to be saved and You've already provided for their salvation." Then you can take your authority and start speaking things that need to happen. Since God has to flow through a person, you can pray according to Romans 10:17 and say, "Father, Your Word says that faith comes by hearing Your Word. So I'm praying that Your Word will come across their path."

> Pray ye therefore the Lord of the harvest, that he will send forth labourers into his harvest.
>
> MATTHEW 9:38

Then pray, "I ask that You would send forth laborers across their path. I believe that right now someone is coming to them to share Your Word. If they're in a bar, let a preacher walk in and give them the Gospel. If they're at home watching television, I pray that they would come across the Word being presented in a program. If they're driving their car, let them turn the radio on to someone sharing the good news. Father, I ask You to send laborers across their path at their job. May a coworker sit down next to them and start telling them how much You love them and how they can be born again."

Remember the Word

Pray that the Word they've already heard will come back to their remembrance.

> But the Comforter, which is the Holy Ghost, whom the Father will send in my name, he shall teach you all things, and bring all things to your remembrance, whatsoever I have said unto you.
>
> JOHN 14:26

Say, "Father, I pray that the Word they heard when they were a kid in Sunday school would come back to them." Somehow, they must receive the incorruptible seed of the Word.

Then, offer yourself as a vessel. It's very ineffective to pray, "Oh God, send laborers across their path," if you're not willing to be one. If you have an opportunity to tell them the truth, take it. I recognize that in certain instances and for whatever reason that person may have just totally cut you off. Maybe there are certain things that this person won't let you talk to them about. However, if you can speak to them, then do so.

If I was praying for God to bring the Word to someone and then, as I was praying, the Lord said, "You go talk to them," I would stop my prayer right there and go talk to that person. Maybe I'd have to call them on the phone, but somehow I would act on God's leading right then. I wouldn't pray about it anymore until I had done as He instructed me to do.

Stand Against the Devil

Also, you can take your authority and stand against the devil.

> In whom the god of this world hath blinded the minds of them which believe not, lest the light of the glorious gospel of Christ, who is the image of God, should shine unto them.
>
> 2 CORINTHIANS 4:4

This verse reveals that a demonic power operates in people who don't believe, blinding them to the truth so that the light of the Gospel won't shine unto them. God needs someone in a physical body to take their authority and release His power, saying, "I command this demonic blindness and hardened heart to be gone in Jesus' name."

Now, I need to clarify something here. Because you are praying for another person who has their own free will, you may need to pray these things for them again and again. This isn't praying in unbelief because they may be negating your prayer by exercising their own free will. Let's say you pray for this person, breaking the blindness and hardness of heart. God opens up their heart, and all of a sudden this deception is gone and the Word is coming to them. They're remembering scriptures and people are coming across their path. Still, if that person isn't ready to repent and receive, they'll reject this conviction and drawing of the Holy Spirit. Their own free will has more power and authority over them than you do. So even though you've prayed for them and you know it's working, they have the right to reject Christ. If they do, then you have to pray that prayer again. It's not that you prayed one of those prayers in unbelief. You believe that your prayer was answered, and it was, but the person just hasn't responded yet.

Pray in faith again, releasing your faith for God to minister to them and break that blindness so they can see Christ. Hopefully, as they are hit with the Gospel a number of times, it will eventually penetrate and begin to soak in. The reason you have to pray this kind of prayer over and over again is due to the fact that the other person is constantly voiding your prayer by hardening their heart.

Remit Their Sins

Another way you can pray for this person is to remit their sins.

> Whose soever sins ye remit, they are remitted unto them; and whose soever sins ye retain, they are retained.
>
> JOHN 20:23

Contrary to what some people have taught, this doesn't mean you can forgive someone of their sins. You don't have the power to forgive sins. However, you can remit them.

When someone with cancer is symptom free, they'll say they are in remission. *Remission* doesn't mean that the cancer is gone, just that there are no visible or physical signs of it. So when the Word says that you can remit sins, it means you can deal with the effects sin causes in that person.

In praying for a lost person, you can break off the demonic blindness and hardness of heart. You can pray that laborers would bring God's Word across their path and that it would come back to their remembrance. You can also remit their sins. All of these are biblical and effective ways to pray. Even though they may choose to resist and reject the drawing of the Holy Spirit, you can be confident that through your prayers God is continuing to work in their life.

CHAPTER 14

How Does Revival Come?

When revival is experienced people are completely in love with God. There's a freshness, a vitality, and an excitement about their relationship with the Lord Jesus Christ. In revival, the miraculous power of God is in manifestation—people are being healed, delivered, saved, and baptized in the Holy Spirit. Churches are full and growing, and folks from all walks of life are turning back to God.

Although I agree that we need revival, it's not going to come the way most people are presently pursuing it. Most people teach that to get revival, we must plead with God, bombard heaven, and grab hold of the horns of the altar, shaking it until God comes out. They tell us that we have to "make" God pour out revival. That's simply not true.

Not a New Testament Prayer

God is much more motivated to send revival than you are to receive it. He longs to see this nation (and the rest of the world) revived and wholeheartedly following Him. He desires to see us yielding to the Holy Spirit and applying godly principles from the Word to our lives. The Lord wants us living in revival much more than we do.

You aren't going to somehow or another get God up to speed with you. That's not what it's about. Yet, so much of what is currently being said concerning prayer for revival is all about us begging God to pour out this and pleading with Him to send that. It's actually these "intercessors" that are praying for revival who are getting a tremendous amount of the credit. From their perspective, if they weren't "standing in the gap," God would just fold His arms and let the whole world go to hell. They don't believe He cares. They think they're causing Him to "repent" by praying, "Oh God, repent. Turn back to us."

Please don't misunderstand. I used to think that way too. For several years, I begged and pleaded with God for revival with all my heart. I'm not saying that the people who do this are all wrong. Many of them see our genuine need for revival, and they long to see God's power manifest. They're just trying to receive it based on the faulty model they've been given.

Most of these people assume that God is so ticked off at us that He's holding back His Holy Spirit. Since mankind (or the church, as it may apply) has moved so far away from what God wants us to do, they perceive Him as having turned His back on us. It's like His arms are folded and He's saying, "I've given you over. Forget you!" They picture God with this attitude, and so they beg Him, "Please, pour out Your Spirit on us. Let Your Holy Spirit fall on us again!" And the intercessors jump in there, praying, "Oh God, have mercy on us. Oh, Lord, don't impute our many sins unto us. We're asking You for mercy—mercy!" They're begging God to turn back to the church and pleading with Him to have mercy on the human race. This is *not* a New Testament prayer!

Moses

The first few verses of 1 Timothy 2 talk about praying for kings, and all those in authority. Then, in verse 5, the Word says:

> There is one God, and one mediator between God and men, the man Christ Jesus.

There is now only one mediator—the Lord Jesus Christ.

A *mediator* is someone who stands between two parties that are at odds with each other, seeking to reconcile them. In the Old Testament, there was a gap between God and man. Sin had separated us, so mediators—like Moses—were needed. Galatians 3:19 says that the Old Testament law was…

> Ordained by angels in the hand of a mediator [Moses[1]].

Moses stood between an angry God and a sinful people. In Exodus 32:12, he prayed:

> Turn from thy fierce wrath, and repent of this evil [You have threatened to do] against thy people.

That's a strong statement. God was told to repent by one of His creations. It's hard to comprehend, but that's exactly what Moses said. "Repent, O God, and turn from Your fierce wrath!" What's even more amazing is, "The LORD repented" (v. 14).

"It Is Finished"

Moses stood as a mediator between an angry God and a sinful people. This worked under the Old Covenant because God was angry. Sin had separated mankind from Him, and there was a judgment to be paid. Therefore, it was appropriate for Moses to mediate. However, now that we're in the New Covenant, Jesus has become our Mediator. (Heb. 7.)

> There is one God, and one mediator between God and men, the man Christ Jesus.
>
> 1 TIMOTHY 2:5

Jesus forever stood in between a holy God and an unholy people. He paid for our sins on the cross and took upon Himself all the wrath and punishment due us from God. This isn't only temporary until the next time you sin, it's forever. He paid for all sin for all time—past, present, and even future tense sin. (Heb. 10:10–14.) Christ has forever reconciled God and man and has brought the two into an eternal union and harmony. (2 Cor. 5:18–19.) Whosoever will may receive this gift of God. When Jesus said on the cross, "It is finished," He was speaking of God's wrath against sin and sinners. (John 19:30.)

So, if Moses were to stand up today and pray, "Repent, O God, and turn from Your fierce wrath," that would be anti-Christ. It would be standing against and trying to take the place of what Christ has done. Moses' ministry of mediation was appropriate in the Old Testament because Jesus hadn't yet come. But now that He has come, for us to pray, "Repent, O God. Don't pour out Your wrath on this city, nation, or people. Have mercy on us," is anti-Christ. You are trying to take the place of Christ and accomplish what He's already done.

The way that much of the church has been praying and pleading with God is literally against what Jesus Christ came to do. It's anti-Christ. A lack of understanding of the New Testament has caused many people to pray for revival the way that they do. Revival doesn't come by begging God. It comes by recognizing that God loves people more than we do and understanding that He wants us revived much more than even we do. We need to stop begging God to pour out His Spirit while passively waiting on a lightning bolt from heaven. Instead, we need to praise the Lord that He wants these results even more than we do. We need to believe God's Word and release our authority by going out and preaching the Gospel.

All the Revival You Can Handle

If you go out and raise someone from the dead, you'll have all the revival you can handle. *But Andrew, you can't raise a person from the dead unless you already have revival!* I disagree. God isn't holding back the flow of His Spirit, we are. It's the body of Christ who are clogging up the pipes and keeping God from flowing. What you need to do is work on your pipe.

You need to work on yourself, saying, "Father, please forgive me for my unbelief. Forgive me for not doing what Your Word says. You said that we're supposed to go and heal the sick, cleanse the lepers, and raise the dead. I've been asking You to pour out Your Spirit and do these things without me. I've been pleading with You to move sovereignly. Please forgive me for that." Then get up, take the Word, and start meditating on it. Once you see on the inside—with the eyes of your heart—blind eyes and deaf ears opened, demons cast out, and the dead raised, then you'll start seeing it manifest in the physical realm too. You'll have revival.

If you start seeing the sick regularly healed, they'll begin breaking holes in the roof to get to you. (Mark 2:4.) If your shadow healed the sick it touched (Acts 5:15–16), there would be so many people crowding around that you'd have all the revival you can handle.

I'm a revivalist. I am seeing people revived—blind eyes and deaf ears opened, terminal diseases healed, demons cast out, the dead raised, and people born again and baptized in the Holy Spirit. All around the world, I'm seeing millions of people's lives being changed. But I'm not asking God to do it. I'm praying, "Lord, I know You desire revival. Please help me to be the vessel of Your love and power that I need to be." I yield myself to Him, praying and fellowshipping with Him, allowing Him to transform me by His Word and His presence. Then I go out and speak the Word of God. I command healings and miracles to manifest, and I'm seeing revival. People are being revived.

I receive emails daily from Asia, Africa, and Europe testifying how different people have been revived. They're changed by God's Word and the power of the Holy Spirit. It's not because I'm begging God in some prayer closet. He's not up in heaven with His arms folded, saying, "Beg a little harder. Get another hundred thousand people to pray. And unless you all fast twice a week, I won't do it!" No, it's not like that. God is in heaven with His arms out, trying to release His power, saying, "Is there anyone who will believe Me? Is there anyone who will stand up and start speaking, living, and demonstrating My Word?" If you will do that, you'll have all the revival you can handle. You'll see people's lives begin to change.

Diana of the Ephesians

The way many people are praying, it seems like we have no influence, no authority, and no power to make God's kingdom come to pass here on this earth. We just approach Him like a beggar, "Oh God, please move. Please have mercy. And please touch us." That isn't accomplishing anything good. It's just making us bitter and angry wondering "Why hasn't God moved? How come He hasn't poured out His Spirit? Why is God allowing this to go on? Why did He let this person die without first being saved?" God isn't letting this happen. He isn't the One allowing our country to go to hell in a handbasket. God didn't make America basically a "post-Christian" nation. It's not God who hasn't poured out His Spirit. The problem is His people who have been begging Him to do what He told us to do. We haven't taken Him at His Word. We haven't been operating in our authority. We've shirked our responsibility by trying to throw it all back on God. This isn't the model we see in the New Testament.

In the New Testament, Jesus never told us to plead with God to heal or to pour out His Spirit. You can't find an example where the Lord conducted His ministry that way. The apostle Peter didn't either.

There's no example of the apostle Paul ever asking his people to "intercede" and tear down the stronghold of Diana of the Ephesians. This temple at Ephesus was one of the seven wonders of the world. They had over one thousand priestesses who had physical relations with the men as they came in to worship. As you might guess, the place was normally packed with people. Paul didn't try to do anything political. He didn't organize the church to pray, begging and pleading that God would stop this idol worship. They didn't get together and do "spiritual warfare," binding and rebuking Diana of the Ephesians. What did Paul do? He preached and demonstrated the Gospel.

Paul told them, "Diana of the Ephesians isn't anything. This statue didn't fall from Jupiter. Diana is no god. There's only one true God, and His Son is the Lord Jesus Christ." Paul did the same thing in Corinth, another Roman city known for multiple idols and immoral worship. He preached the truth, and God used that truth to set people free. Paul didn't organize "intercessors" to cover every zone in the region. He didn't have people do "spiritual warfare" or "spiritual mapping." These things that are being done today by the church in an effort to try to change our nation are not what Jesus commanded us to do in the Word of God.

The New Testament Example

In the New Testament, the believers went out and preached the Word everywhere.

> They went forth, and preached every where, the Lord working with them, and confirming the word with signs following.
>
> MARK 16:20

They proclaimed and demonstrated God's Word. As they preached the truth, the Holy Spirit bore supernatural witness to that truth. So many people repented and converted to Christ that the temple of Diana in Ephesus fell into disrepair. The people forsook it because they turned from her to God. Diana of the Ephesians hasn't even been a factor in two thousand years until the "intercessors" resurrected her a few years ago with what they call "spiritual warfare."

I'm not trying to be mean—I just want to challenge your thinking with God's Word. Show me in the New Testament where we are to send people to foreign countries to do nothing but pray and tear down spiritual strongholds. Show me in the Word of God where it says we should send people on mission trips but forbid them to preach the Gospel, saying, "Don't witness because you might get censored, punished, or persecuted." That's what is being done today. We are spending millions of dollars to send people to foreign countries just to let them walk around and pray. You can't find a scriptural model for this stuff. You might be able to twist and pervert a verse or two, but if you just take the Word at face value—reading it and believing it as is—you can't find any examples of this.

What you can find, however, is scripture where believers prayed for boldness.

> Now, Lord, behold their threatenings: and grant unto thy servants, that with all boldness they may speak thy word, by stretching forth thine hand to heal; and that signs and wonders may be done by the name of thy holy child Jesus.
>
> ACTS 4:29,30

Paul asked his friends to pray that he'd be bold despite his challenging circumstances.

> Praying…for me, that utterance may be given unto me, that I may open my mouth boldly, to make known the mystery of the gospel, for which I am an ambassador in bonds: that therein I may speak boldly, as I ought to speak.
>
> EPHESIANS 6:18–20

The early New Testament believers prayed that they would be bold, faithful witnesses despite opposition, but they didn't ask God to just "sovereignly" pour out His Spirit on unbelievers without them preaching, demonstrating, and doing their part. There simply isn't a scriptural example for that. Basically, that's the reason the church isn't having more of a salt and light influence on our generation. We aren't really following the New Testament example.

The Power of God

When Jesus gave power and authority to the church, it came with responsibility. We need to use our authority and preach God's Word. We need to speak the truth to the people the Lord has put in our lives. As they receive that truth into their hearts, their lives will be changed. Many people have rejected the preaching they've heard because it wasn't the true Gospel. It was just powerless religion and lifeless tradition. It was just condemnation and judgment. That's not the message of the Gospel. We need to preach the good news of salvation by faith in the Lord Jesus Christ. The Gospel is the power of God. (Rom. 1:16.)

My teaching entitled *Grace, the Power of the Gospel* (in audio as "The Gospel: The Power of God") takes a closer look at this very issue. The book of Romans is the apostle Paul's masterpiece on the grace of God. In it, he clearly reveals what is the Gospel—this powerful good news message we are to preach.

CHAPTER 15

Believe and Receive

As believers in the Lord Jesus Christ, it's our responsibility to boldly preach the Gospel and faithfully teach God's Word.

> Whosoever shall call upon the name of the Lord shall be saved. How then shall they call on him in whom they have not believed? and how shall they believe in him of whom they have not heard? and how shall they hear without a preacher? And how shall they preach, except they be sent? as it is written, How beautiful are the feet of them that preach the gospel of peace, and bring glad tidings of good things...So then faith cometh by hearing, and hearing by the word of God.
>
> ROMANS 10:13–15,17

The manifestation of the Holy Spirit on the day of Pentecost arrested the people's attention. Seizing the opportunity, Peter stood up and preached Christ. The people responded by asking, "What must we do to be saved?" Peter answered:

> Repent, and be baptized every one of you in the name of Jesus Christ for the remission of sins, and ye shall receive the gift of the Holy Ghost. For *the promise* is unto you, and to your children, and to all that are afar off, even as many as the Lord our God shall call.
>
> ACTS 2:38,39

Considering the context—the day of Pentecost—and looking back to Acts 1:4–5 and 8, it's clear that the promise being spoken of here is the outpouring of the Holy Spirit. Almost everyone would agree that the outpouring of the Holy Spirit is part and parcel of true revival. Peter was saying, "What You've seen—this outpouring of the Holy Spirit, this manifestation of the coming of God's Spirit, the indwelling of the Holy Ghost, and the miraculous manifestations this has caused—is not only for you, but also for your children, for your children's children, and all those who will follow." Peter was looking into the future to the generations to come, saying that this promise they were experiencing of the outpoured Holy Spirit is for us today too.

Tarrying for the Holy Spirit

God never quit pouring out His Holy Spirit. This promise was intended to go from generation to generation to all believers throughout time. Although the baptism in the Holy Spirit and the gifts of the Holy Spirit have only been widely recognized and received by the body of Christ at large for the last century or so, it's not because they weren't available. An honest look at church history will reveal pockets of believers down through the centuries ever since the book of Acts who received the Holy Spirit and operated in His power. However, somewhere along the way—perhaps around the beginning of what's now called the Dark Ages—the church at large, for whatever reasons, stopped believing for and receiving this promise.

In the early days of Azusa Street[1] and the beginning of the Pentecostal movement, these believers didn't fully understand how they received this powerful manifestation of the Holy Spirit. They didn't understand exactly what they did—or if they did anything at all—to occasion it. As a result, one of dominant doctrines that emerged from those early days of the Pentecostal movement was to "tarry" for the Holy Spirit. They said, "You have to beg and plead with God to pour out and fill you with His Holy Spirit." They would just wait—sometimes years—for this cataclysmic experience where God would touch them and baptize them in the Holy Spirit.

It's almost as if we've swung over to the opposite extreme today. Many people come forward who have never even heard about the baptism in the Holy Spirit. When the minister asks if they'd like to receive, they answer, "Well, I guess so." They don't know why they need the Holy Spirit. They don't know what to expect. There's no anticipation and no desire. I've seen people receive prayer for the baptism in the Holy Spirit, walk back to their seat, and it seems to have zero impact on their life. That's not good either. It shouldn't be that way.

One good thing about the way the old-time Pentecostals did it was that when they finally received the baptism in the Holy Spirit, it meant something to them. They would pray desperately, wailing and travailing before God, sometimes for years. But once received, the Holy Spirit had a profound impact on their lives.

We know today that we don't have to "tarry" or wait for God to pour out His Spirit. We don't have to beg and plead for the Lord to send the Holy Ghost. We can just believe and receive the free gift He's given. Still, it would be wonderful to see the hunger that the "tarrying" produced.

Go to Jerusalem

In Acts 1, Jesus told His disciples to wait for the baptism of the Holy Spirit.

> Being assembled together with them, [Jesus] commanded them that they should not depart from Jerusalem, but wait for the promise of the Father...ye shall be baptized with the Holy Ghost not many days hence.
>
> ACTS 1:4,5

At the time, Jesus had resurrected, but He hadn't yet ascended. He was still bodily upon the earth. Soon after He ascended though, He poured out the Holy Spirit on His disciples on the day of Pentecost. Now that the Holy Spirit has already been given, there's no need to wait any longer.

In light of that, if you're going to take this admonition to wait literally, then you must also physically go to the city of Jerusalem to do it.

> Behold, I send the promise of my Father upon you: but tarry ye in the city of Jerusalem, until ye be endued with power from on high.
>
> LUKE 24:49

> [Jesus] commanded them that they should not depart from Jerusalem, but wait for the promise of the Father.
>
> ACTS 1:4

Jesus told these disciples to wait because there was about fifty more days until Pentecost. That's not the case anymore. Now that the Holy Spirit has already been poured out, you can just believe and receive.

I've seen thousands and thousands of people pray for and receive the baptism in the Holy Spirit, speak in tongues, and have a life-changing experience with God right away simply by believing and receiving. You don't have to wait and "tarry."

"We've Got It"

Most people would agree with what I'm sharing about the baptism in the Holy Spirit, but when it comes to revival, they just shift gears saying, "Oh, but we have to beg and plead, wail and travail. We must get a million people praying and fasting together so God will send revival and pour out His Spirit." No, you just have to believe. You just have to receive. And as you get revived, you'll have an opportunity to influence and share that revival with the people around you. As you, your friends, your family, and your workplace get revived, they go out and share too, and it spreads.

The reason we aren't seeing a greater revival isn't because we don't have millions of people praying and asking God to pour out His Spirit. It's simply that we have very few people who are flowing in revival—believing God's Word, taking their authority, and making the power of God manifest.

Duncan Campbell, an outstanding Scottish preacher in the early to mid-twentieth century, preached the Scottish Hebrides Revival. This was a powerful manifestation of the Holy Spirit that was received over a hundred years ago. I actually heard him speak when he was older. He told how there were two little Scottish women who prayed for over twenty years; then there was a Scottish pastor and his seven elders who also prayed nearly a year, all asking the Lord to pour out His Spirit. Finally, one day the power of God hit, and they experienced all of these glorious things. He said this happened because of all that begging and pleading with God for over twenty years.

Several years after hearing that, I heard the testimony of a man who as a young man had showed up at that final prayer meeting right before the power hit. He said that these other men had prayed every Saturday night for almost a year. They were begging God for an outpouring of His Spirit. This young man walked in, prayed until two in the morning, and declared, "Either God's Word is true, or it isn't. We've got it. I'm going home."

The revival actually came when they quit begging and started believing. Once they started believing God's Word that revival was theirs, everything changed and the power was loosed. We've been given power and authority by the Lord. We must step out in faith and use what God has given us, or revival won't manifest.

Silence

Imagine that you've given me your Bible. It's a gift, and it's in my possession right now. What would you do if I turned to you and asked, "May I please borrow your Bible? I'd like to look up a scripture. I really need to hear from God, and I believe He's speaking to me. Would you please give me your Bible?" I could beg. I could plead. I could even try to condemn you, saying, "If you were really a Christian, you'd share your Bible with me." What would you do? You've already given it to me.

How do you respond to someone who is asking you to give them something they've already got? How do you answer somebody who is begging you to do something you've already done for them? If I was the one being asked those questions, I'm not sure how I'd respond. Probably, I'd just look at them dumbfounded. I wouldn't say anything.

If someone is asking for something they already have, how does a person respond to that? Probably in silence. Sounds a lot like the way God has responded to all of our begging and pleading for an outpouring of the Holy Spirit.

The truth is, God poured out His Holy Spirit on the day of Pentecost, and He's never withdrawn Him since. (Acts 2:38–39.) The Lord has never become so ticked off that He just said, "Alright, Holy Spirit. Come on back. No more revival. No more manifestations." God didn't cause the church to go through the Dark Ages. He didn't will that there be a period of time where truth would be so bound up that very few would ever see it. God didn't just all of a sudden—"sovereignly"—reach down and touch Martin Luther. He didn't just decide to pour out His Spirit upon the reformers to do something "new" because, after all, God was tired of a thousand years worth of deadness in the earth. No, the problem wasn't God's giving—it was our believing and receiving.

Waves?

Martin Luther had a real heart for God. He wasn't satisfied with the religious teaching and traditionally accepted doctrine of his day. As a pilgrim to the holy city, praying his rosary and climbing up the steps of the holy building, he realized that visiting that place and doing those things didn't make any difference. As he stood there, fed up with it all, the Holy Spirit brought scripture back to his remembrance.

> Where is boasting then? It is excluded. By what law? of works? Nay: but by the law of faith. Therefore we conclude that a man is justified by faith without the deeds of the law.
>
> ROMANS 3:27,28

Martin Luther heard the Word and believed it. Then he acted on it by nailing his ninety-five theses up on the door of his church in Wittenburg, Germany. He stood boldly before the religious leaders at the Diet of Worms, giving his defense. Martin Luther proclaimed the Word of God, and that Word acted like wildfire in the hungry hearts of the people. From it, the Reformation sprung up and the world was forever changed. This wasn't because God just sovereignly said, "Alright, I'm ready to do something new on the earth." No, it was because a single person—a physical human being—believed, received, and acted on the Word of God.

Religion teaches that God moves in waves. Back in the 1940s and 50s, there was the healing movement that came through the body of Christ. There were healing revivals, healing evangelists, and tent meetings springing up everywhere. Then there was the charismatic movement and the Word of Faith movement. Now there's this and that movement, and people are saying, "Look, God is doing a new thing! He's pouring out His Spirit again." No, that's not how God works.

The healing revival sprung up because someone saw healing in the Word, believed God, and started releasing this power into the earth by using their authority. They stepped out in faith on the Word and saw the Holy Spirit demonstration. That healing power has been available ever since the death, burial, and resurrection of Christ, but the church just hadn't been receiving it.

Always Available

Back in the 1940s, most of the church believed that miracles, signs, and wonders had all passed away with the apostles. This was the dominant theological position being taught. However, a young man named Oral Roberts received healing from tuberculosis and stuttering after being bedridden for over five months. As he studied the Word, he became personally convinced that it's God's will to heal today. So this young minister stepped out on that Word by renting a hall in Enid, Oklahoma.

In this first meeting, Oral asked God for three things. The first was a certain minimum number of people in attendance. So before he ever even went out on the stage, Oral stood behind the curtain and counted the people. Then he went out and immediately took up an offering. Oral had told God, "I'm not going to go in debt, so if this is You, You're going to have to bring in enough money to at least cover these expenses." After the offering was counted, the second requirement was met—nearly to the penny. The third thing Oral asked for was at least one notable miracle. He said, "God, I'm going to preach and proclaim that it's still Your will to heal today. If this is really You, then we have to see at least one notable miracle." After preaching his sermon, he called people forward and the healings began to manifest. From then on, it was full steam ahead.

Oral Roberts—and many others—began proclaiming the Word of God concerning healing. As people believed that Word and received healing, a revival broke out. Some people think, *Well, God just sovereignly moved.* No, the Lord has always desired for us to receive healings, manifest miracles, and experience revival ever since He walked on this earth. Jesus Himself said:

> Verily, verily, I say unto you, He that believeth on me, the works that I do shall he do also; and greater works than these shall he do; because I go unto my Father.
>
> John 14:12

We can debate what the "greater works" are, but what are you going to do with "the works that I do shall he do also"?

God always intended for His church to operate in the supernatural. It's not God that just skipped from around 200 A.D. until 1940. No, it's people who quit appropriating His power. Christians got into unbelief. They stopped operating in faith. Finally, somebody broke through this barrier and started believing again. Then they preached and proclaimed God's Word. When they took their authority and used it, healing manifested. Yet, the whole counsel of God has always been available to those who would believe.

God doesn't just move for a decade in this and then move for a decade in that. "Ten years ago He moved in healing. Now He's forgotten healing, and is moving in righteousness. This next decade He's going to work on marriages. There's a new wave coming!" Nonsense. That's just man's attempt to justify our powerlessness.

Work on Your Receiver

The Lord is today all that He ever was and all that He'll ever be.

> Jesus Christ the same yesterday, and to day, and for ever.
>
> HEBREWS 13:8

He wants to move in and through your life in miracles, healings, deliverance, and prosperity. Everything that God is, is now available to you through His Word. You don't have to beg and plead, and then just passively sit back and wait to see what God will do. The Bible calls that unbelief.

> Without faith it is impossible to please him: for he that cometh to God must believe that he is, and that he is a rewarder of them that diligently seek him.
>
> HEBREWS 11:6

God honors those who honor Him. (see 1 Sam. 1; 2:20–21.) Believe that God is. He's a rewarder of those who diligently seek Him. Pray, "Father, I am seeking You. Your Word tells me that You have provided all these things. By faith, I receive. Thank You, Lord!" As you seek Him and continue building yourself up in faith, the power of God will manifest and you'll operate in all the revival you want. You're the one who determines how much revival you have—not God.

You don't have to pray and just passively wait, saying, "I've been praying twenty years for revival and we haven't got it yet. I don't know why God hasn't done it." That's just as wrong as someone saying, "I've been praying twenty years for the baptism in the Holy Spirit, but God hasn't given it to me yet." No, God has already given; you just haven't received it yet. It's not God's *giver* that's having the problem—it's your *receiver.* You need to work on your receiving, not God's giving.

CHAPTER 16

God Has Given You Power

> God created man in his own image, in the image of God created he him; male and female created he them. And God blessed them, and God said unto them, Be fruitful, and multiply, and replenish the earth, and subdue it: and have dominion over the fish of the sea, and over the fowl of the air, and over every living thing that moveth upon the earth.
>
> GENESIS 1:27,28

The Lord blessed us and gave us the ability to procreate. He said to Adam and Eve, "You be fruitful. You multiply. You replenish the earth." This power and authority God gave us came with responsibility.

The Lord gave us the ability to create children. He doesn't send them to us via some stork. It's God's power, but He set certain things in motion. So, you can pray until you're blue in the face, but a woman isn't going to get pregnant until she has a relationship with a man. That's the way God intended this to operate, and that's the way it works.

Our Responsibility

If someone was just praying and praying and praying to be pregnant and have a child, yet they had no physical relationship with a man, we'd look at them and think, *How dumb can you get and still breathe? Didn't anybody tell her the facts of life? Don't they understand how things work?* Yet this is exactly what many Christians are doing in other areas of life.

They are asking God for healing, but they aren't doing what the Word says. God's Word says to speak to your mountain.

> Whosoever shall say unto this mountain, Be thou removed, and be thou cast into the sea; and shall not doubt in his heart, but shall believe that those things which he saith shall come to pass; he shall have whatsoever he saith.
>
> MARK 11:23

That's one of God's laws. Yet, people aren't doing what the Word says and they wonder *Why hasn't God healed me yet?* That's just as foolish as a woman who prays constantly to get pregnant without having any relationship with a man, and then when nothing happens, says, "Why hasn't God given me a child yet?" God gave us power and authority in this area.

With this power and authority comes responsibility. I know a couple who had twelve kids. When I asked the husband, "How many children are you going to have?" he answered, "If God wants us to have kids, we'll have kids. It's just totally up to God." There are certain forms of birth control that I don't advocate because in actuality they are abortion, but if nothing else a little self-control would help. If you don't exercise some self-control in this area, thinking, *If it's God's will, we'll have children. But if it's not, we won't,* then you're totally ignoring your responsibility. God blessed us and gave us power to procreate.

If people never had children unless it was God's will, then prostitutes wouldn't get pregnant. If all children were just supernaturally ordained of God, unwed mothers wouldn't conceive. It's not God's will for people who aren't married to bear children. If God was directly controlling this aspect of our lives, He wouldn't let children be born addicted to drugs or with HIV. God gave power to procreate to physical human beings, and if you cooperate with how He made this universe to function, you can create a child.

We Must Cooperate

Creation of human life is God's power, but He put it under our control. We have power and authority in this area. If you want the results, then you have to do the right things to cooperate with those laws of how to conceive and birth children. Most people understand this, and they would ridicule someone who thinks they can just pray for a child to appear. God doesn't just supernaturally drop children out of heaven. That's not how they come.

Just praying and asking God to supernaturally drop healing, salvation, or revival from heaven is not how they come. There are spiritual laws that we must use our authority as human beings to cooperate with. If we don't step out in faith to cooperate with God in these areas, they won't come to pass.

This is so simple that you'd have to have somebody help you to misunderstand it. Yet, we've had a lot of help. I've talked to many people who have asked, "If God is really God, then He could have healed this person. Why did He let them die?"

God isn't like that. He doesn't just say, "Alright, you have power to heal. You go out and heal the sick." Then—if we aren't doing it because we don't know or because we're more dominated by unbelief than faith—God doesn't just look down and say, "These folks are never going to get the job done. Since they're not believing My Word or doing it the way I said, I'm just going to heal this person anyway." That would violate His own integrity.

God told us, "we have the power. We are to go out. We are to heal the sick, cleanse the lepers, raise the dead." (Matt. 10:8.) If we don't do our part, God isn't going to step in and do what He's told us to do. No amount of begging or pleading will change that situation. We in the body of Christ need to discover what God has given to us. We need to find out what's under our authority and start using it the way God intended. Let's take our responsibility and lay aside our unbelief. Let's reject all these religious doctrines that absolve us of our responsibility and say, "Whatever will be, will be. It's just up to God who gets saved and healed. He does all things sovereignly." Let's stop backing out of our responsibility and placing the blame on God. He's not the one failing—it's us.

Power to Get Wealth

In the area of provision, God has given us power to get wealth.

> Thou shalt remember the LORD thy God: for it is he that giveth thee power to get wealth, that he may establish his covenant which he sware unto thy fathers, as it is to this day.
>
> DEUTERONOMY 8:18

Anytime God gives us power, He also gives us authority so we can release the power and use it. With this authority comes responsibility. This is why God doesn't give us money directly. The scripture doesn't say that God gives us money. He gave us power—an anointing, an ability—to get wealth.

First of all, God doesn't have money. He doesn't use money. In heaven, there is no currency of exchange. Neither does He make money. If you're praying, "Oh God, I need $100," or whatever currency it is that you need, God doesn't have any of those bills, and He's not going to counterfeit them either. He's not going to make money and put it in your pocket. The Bible says:

> Give, and it shall be given unto you; good measure, pressed down, and shaken together, and running over, shall *men* give into your bosom.
>
> LUKE 6:38

Since God doesn't have money directly, He sends it to you through people. God impresses other people, and people will be involved in getting you His supply.

The Work of Your Hands

Many people are ignorant of this truth. Some of them pray, "God, if you're God, You can do anything. Put money in my wallet." Then they open up their wallet, and when there's no more money in there than before, they say, "Well, God isn't faithful. The Word doesn't work. It's just not true." Then they start blaming God out of their ignorance.

God isn't going to create money and put it in your wallet. God gave you power to get wealth, so you must learn to use your authority to release that power. In order to see God's provision for you manifest, you must cooperate with the spiritual laws governing prosperity.

For additional information on this topic, I recommend my teachings entitled, *Financial Stewardship, Blessings and Miracles,* and *The Power of Partnership.*

God has promised to bless all the work of your hands.

> The LORD shall command the blessing upon thee...in all that thou settest thine hand unto...The LORD shall...bless all the work of thine hand.
>
> DEUTERONOMY 28:8,12

However, if you aren't setting your hands to something, God doesn't have anything to bless. You can't just sit at home doing nothing and expect the Lord to prosper you. It doesn't work that way. You aren't going to see God begin to prosper you if you aren't working. In fact, the Word says:

> This we commanded you, that if any would not work, neither should he eat.
>
> 2 THESSALONIANS 3:10

"Go Get a Job Until"

God is into work. He's into you doing something productive. That's why welfare—as it's currently being practiced in our country—isn't a godly concept. I'm not saying that any person who's receiving welfare is ungodly. I'm not saying that God hates them, or they're in sin. But I am saying that it isn't God's system.

Anyone might need help on occasion. There's nothing wrong with you taking the help of other people or a government if you are in a situation where you temporarily need it. But to be a second, third, or fourth generation welfare recipient where you just sit at home and let the government pay you for doing nothing is an ungodly concept.

If you're going to get into God's divine flow of provision, then you need to start doing some things to release that power and see this anointing begin to generate the income you need. God has given you the power to get wealth, but you need to do something. You need to work. You need to set your hand to something productive.

One of our partners worked as the CEO of a corporation then suddenly his company downsized and he was laid off. He started drawing unemployment and took that for a period of time. He wanted to work, so he put in resumes all over town, but this was during an economically challenging time and he was overqualified. Therefore, no one was hiring him.

When he was a few weeks away from getting his house repossessed and losing everything, he came to me and asked, "What do I do?"

I answered, "Go get a job."

He said, "I'm trying."

I continued, "No, I mean go get a job *until.* There's nothing wrong with you believing for another CEO job or something similar, but until your better paying job comes in, get a job stocking shelves or flipping burgers."

This guy was highly offended. "I'm a CEO. I couldn't do something like that. Besides, I need more money than that. My house is about to be repossessed." He was something like $5,000 behind, and hadn't worked in over a year.

I told him, "If you would have been stocking shelves or flipping burgers for the past year, you would have had enough money to keep this house from being repossessed while you still sought the job you're believing for. There's nothing wrong with you not wanting to stay there, but you've got to do something. By doing nothing, you are abdicating your responsibility and keeping the blessing God wants to give you from manifesting.

"You can pray and pray, and you might get a miracle that will tide you over to the next week or month. But then you'll have another crisis next month, and the month after that, and the month after that. You aren't going to see the supernatural flow of finances start manifesting in your life until you recognize God gave you power and authority to get wealth. You need to stand up and use that power and authority by doing something."

Thimble or Bucket?

Many people are waiting on their ship to come in, but they've never sent one out. They're waiting on a crop to grow up, but they haven't sown any seed. They're believing God for a great supply, but they haven't cooperated with His spiritual laws concerning prosperity. Remember, the Word says:

> Give, and it shall be given unto you; good measure, pressed down, and shaken together, and running over, shall men give into your bosom. For with the same measure that ye mete withal it shall be measured to you again.
>
> LUKE 6:38

Are you using a tiny little thimble, throwing God five bucks here and there, thinking that you're really being generous, when the truth is the tithe off of your paycheck would be $200, $300, or $400? Are you tipping God and wondering, *How come my finances aren't coming in? I'm praying and believing for prosperity.* The Lord said He would give back to you with the same measure that you used. If you're using a thimble, then He's going to use a thimble to give back to you. And if you need a bucket full of finances, it's going to take a long time for God to measure that back to you with the same measure you gave out.

This is how the kingdom works. God doesn't give you money—He gives you the power to get money. Then there are things you must do to release that power. One of them is to set your hand to something. Stocking shelves or flipping burgers is better than getting welfare. "But Andrew, I'm actually making more money off of welfare than I could working one of those jobs." The difference is, God can't bless welfare, but He can bless stocking shelves or flipping burgers. He could promote you to manager. While there, you could meet someone who could give you a promotion, or even offer you another job. But when you're doing nothing, you're hindering the power of God from flowing in your own life.

It's not God who fails to answer our prayers—it's us who fail to take our authority and use it properly.

CHAPTER 17

The Devil Will Flee From You

> Submit yourselves therefore to God. Resist the devil, and he will flee from you.
>
> JAMES 4:7

God has given us power and authority over the devil.

> Then [Jesus] called his twelve disciples together, and gave them power and authority over *all* devils, and to cure diseases.
>
> LUKE 9:1

God gave us power and authority over *all* devils—and *all* means *all.* There are *no* demons excluded from this. I meet people constantly who say, "Well, the devil is doing this to me, and the devil is doing that." If you know that the devil is your problem, then you can solve that problem by believing God's Word and exercising your authority instead of going around saying, "Oh, God. Please get the devil off my back. Oh, Lord. The devil is trying to cause me to do this." You aren't going to get freed from Satan's harassment by praying and asking God to remove the devil. As we just saw, that power and authority has been given to you.

This first verse doesn't say that he will flee from God. He'll flee from you. It's God's power, but that power is in you. God Himself isn't going to come down and make the devil flee from you. You have to resist the devil.

Satan Is a Coward

Resist means "to actively fight against." Resistance is active.[1] You have to stir yourself up and get mad in the godly sense: the godly use of anger is to be mad at the devil, mad at sickness, mad at disease, and mad at poverty. You have to stir yourself up. You can't just tolerate it. As long as you can tolerate something, you will. But when you get to the place where you say, "I've had it. Enough is enough. This is it," and you rise up with godly anger and faith to exercise your authority, a positive spiritual dynamic is released. When you get sick and tired of being sick and tired and you put your foot down and resist the devil, he flees from you.

For more information about the godly use of anger, please check out my teaching entitled *Anger Management.*

At heart, Satan is a coward. He really is. He's just a bully—intimidating, yelling, and threatening. Even though he says all these things, the truth is he's a coward. If you've ever been around a bully, you'll know that they're always trying to take advantage of other people, manipulating and controlling them. As a boy, I learned that if you stand up to a bully, they'll respect you and leave you alone. You might lose a battle and get beat up, but you'll only fight once. After that, they'll respect you and leave you alone. At heart, a bully doesn't really want to fight. They just want to intimidate and control. If they realize that you're going to stand up and fight every time they come around and try to do something to you, they'll back down. Even if they win the fight, they don't want to put forth that much effort. That's the way Satan is.

When you get angry and resist the devil, he's just like a bully. The moment he knows that it's going to cost him something—that you're going to stand there toe-to-toe in the name of Jesus and go at it with him—Satan will flee from you. But you must resist!

"Dear Devil..."

Saying, "Dear devil, please leave me alone" is not resisting. My friends and I were ministering deliverance once to a woman who had sold her soul to the devil. Satan had led her to do a despicable act involving other people's bodily secretions, among other things, in establishing these demonic pacts. We instructed her that she needed to address the devil and take back the place she had given him. We told her she needed to do this by speaking directly to Satan and renouncing him. So we knelt around a coffee table and started praying. Then we said, "Now you speak to the devil."

This woman said, "Dear devil..." We had to stop her right there and say, "Whoa. Wait a minute. This isn't resisting the devil." You don't resist the devil by saying, "Dear devil, please leave me alone." You must *resist* the devil. God gave you power and authority and you have to activate it by stirring yourself up, becoming violently resolved (Matt. 11:12), and just putting your spiritual foot down by saying, "Satan, get out of my life!" You might be thinking, *But Andrew, I'm just not the assertive type.* The only other option is to suffer. That's just the way it works.

God isn't going to rebuke the devil for you. You have to stand up and resist him. And if you resist the devil, he *will* flee from you. God gave you this authority, and you can't beg Him to do what He's told you to do. It won't work.

Kenneth E. Hagin used to tell the story of how one time, the Lord appeared to him and was giving him instructions. As Jesus was speaking, a little devil started running, jumping, and yelling in between them. Kenneth tried to pay attention and look around this demon, but he couldn't really focus on what the Lord was saying. He wondered why God was allowing this to go on.

Finally, Kenneth became so upset over this that he declared, "In the name of Jesus, I command you to leave!" and this little demon took off and was gone. The Lord looked at Kenneth and said, "If you hadn't have done that, I couldn't."

Two Sides of the Coin

God told you to resist the devil, and he will flee from you. Many Christians know that it's the devil trying to destroy their life today. He's trying to kill you with sickness and disease, or he's stealing your prosperity from you. You know what's happening isn't God's will, but you're praying, "Oh Lord, please solve this. Please do something." You aren't taking your authority. If you are dealing with demonic opposition against you, then you have to step up to the plate, take the authority God has given you, and command the devil to flee.

There are two sides to this coin—submitting to God and resisting the devil. You can't just go around binding and rebuking anything you want. Some people take James 4:7 the wrong way and think things like, *It's the devil who gave me this spouse and I want a new one. So I'm taking authority and commanding my new spouse to come along and to get this one out of the way.* That's not going to happen because God didn't give you that kind of power and authority. Taking your current spouse out of the way (through divorce) so you can marry another isn't His will. You must submit yourself to God and resist the devil, and then he'll flee from you.

These truths concerning authority will only work for you when you're submitted to God. When you are seeking Him with your whole heart and you perceive the devil hindering you, then you can take your authority and command those things to change. If you're just upset because someone cut in front of you in traffic and you say, "I hope they have a wreck down the road," that isn't going to come to pass. God didn't give you authority to curse people like that; you aren't submitted to Him if you do it. But when you are submitted to God, then you can resist the devil—actively fight against him—and he will flee from you.

When I was still in a denominational church, my friends and I stumbled into casting out demons. We saw a woman who normally would have been put into a mental hospital for the rest of her life set free. We knew her problem wasn't physical or natural, but demonic. We also knew that the authorities wouldn't understand, so we locked her in a room for seven days and took shifts ministering to her. We'd praise God, sing songs about the blood of Jesus, and read Scripture. We didn't know what we were doing, but we literally just beat the devil out of this woman—not with our hands, but by singing about the blood and speaking against the devil. We just stayed in there until we saw this woman delivered of demons. Once word got out how she had been restored to her right mind, people started coming to us from all over.

"What's Your Name?"

Another time a homosexual fellow came to us to be delivered. We didn't really know what we were doing, and to make matters worse, we read a book that taught us all kinds of fallacies like, you can't cast out a demon by yourself, you must have two people, you had to get their name, and you must have the person throw up in a bucket. We did some stupid things by following that book's instructions.

We spent three weeks preparing this homosexual for deliverance, which you don't have to do. There's a group in the city where I live who think it's godly to require people seeking deliverance to fill out a forty-page questionnaire and then endure a forty-five day waiting period before they'll cast the demons out. That's not the method Jesus used!

Back when we thought we had to always get the demon's name, a friend of mine who was casting out a demon from someone asked the demon, "What's your name, in Jesus' name?"

The demon answered, "Liar."

Immediately, my friend asked, "Are you telling me the truth?"

"I'm Not Leaving With These Demons"

This homosexual fellow we had been prepping came during a Wednesday night service at our church. I was leading the meeting by myself because the associate pastor, who was my partner in casting out demons, was out of town that night. An usher came and got me out of the service, saying, "This guy wants to see you." When I went back and saw him, he had come with another homosexual who wanted to be delivered too.

The fellow we'd been prepping said, "I'm ready to be delivered tonight."

I answered, "Well, we can't do it tonight. I'm by myself."

He responded, "I'm not leaving with these demons."

"Well, I'm not casting them out."

"You'd better do something because I'm not leaving with these demons."

So I took this man and his friend into a back room in this denominational church. Jamie, who is now my wife but wasn't at the time, came with us to give some prayer support. Jamie wasn't even baptized in the Holy Spirit yet. We had no idea what we were doing.

Once we got to the back room, this man said, "You better plead the blood over this place or do something because these demons are coming out."

When I began praying, "Father, in the name of Jesus," this guy fell to the floor and started barking, slithering like a snake, and throwing chairs up against the glass wall. It was quite a commotion! When the usher heard this, he went in and stopped the service, saying, "We need to pray for Andrew. He's back there witnessing to somebody." They didn't have a clue what was going on.

"Shut Up and Come Out!"

In that back room, there was a stack of chairs about ten high. The other demonized guy was on top of the stack, plastered against the wall, scared to death. Jamie was praying and doing everything she knew to do.

I didn't know how to proceed, but since we were already in it, I started asking, "What's your name? In the name of Jesus, tell me your name." As I went through this, one demon would name itself and then another, and then another. I felt like I was being made a fool because I didn't know if the first demon had come out or not before the second one had named itself. It was ridiculous! Finally, this scripture came to mind.

> Jesus rebuked him, saying, Hold thy peace, and come out of him.
>
> MARK 1:25

I thought, *That would be good.* So I said, "In the name of Jesus, I command you all to shut up and come out of him!" Instantly, power was released and this guy lay on the floor just like he was dead. Gently, I shook him to see if he was okay. He just rolled over and whispered, "I'm free. I'm delivered. I'm free." I thought, *If it's as simple as commanding the demons to come out in Jesus' name, why did I go through all this other stuff?*

Although we didn't know what we were doing, we stumbled onto this truth. We used to beg and plead, asking "Oh, God, please get rid of this." I learned through doing that God has given me authority and I don't have to go through all these things. I don't have to ask the demon's their name, make people fill out a forty-page questionnaire, or require them to wait several weeks to get ready. I have authority over the devil and if the person is willing to cooperate, I can go in and command those demons to leave and they will obey me.

I can't ask God to cast the devil out because that's what He has told me to do. I have to stand up, take my authority, and be confident that when I speak it's going to work. I have to have faith in God's Word—that I do have authority over all devils and to cure diseases. (Luke 9:1.)

Simple Adjustments, Big Difference

Since God has given you this power and authority, you also have the responsibility to exercise it. You can't go back to God and beg Him to do what He has commanded you to do. You must take your authority and use it.

There is no problem with God. Prayer works. It's just that wrong prayer doesn't work. You must pray, speak, and act in line with the authority that God has given you.

If you would just make these simple adjustments that I've been sharing with you throughout this book, you'll see a big difference. Speak to your problems and command God's Word into manifestation. Pray the Word of God across people's paths who need to be born again. Stop begging the Lord for an outpouring of His Spirit, and start going out and healing the sick, cleansing the lepers, and raising the dead. (Matt. 10:8.) Do what the Word says, and you'll see His power manifest. Then you'll have all the revival you can handle.

CHAPTER 18

Law Enforcement

We exercise authority when we take our responsibility and do what God has told us to do. Yet, this doesn't mean we can just "command" anything we want. All authority can do is enforce law.

In the natural realm, we call policemen "law enforcement officers." They only have authority to enforce what's already been established as a law. Police officers don't go out and make up the law. They aren't absolute dictators who can do whatever they want. They are limited. All they can do is enforce laws that are already in effect. It's the same way in the spiritual realm.

Every born-again believer has this supernatural, God-given power. Still, there are spiritual laws governing how it works. Like a police officer, all we can do is enforce the law that's already in effect. We can't use God's power in a selfish way because there isn't any law where God promises to give you what you're lusting for. Instead, we need to learn what the laws of God's kingdom are and then recognize that our authority is simply enforcing these spiritual laws.

In the natural realm, some people try to violate the laws of the land. This is why there's a need for law enforcement officers—people who go out and enforce those laws. In the spiritual realm, there are demons who are constantly trying to oppose us, inflict their evil will upon us, and prevent us from experiencing the fullness of God's provision. We must enforce the spiritual laws of God's kingdom that have been established.

A Legal, Binding Contract

Most people don't see the kingdom of God as operating under law. Instead, they see it as being directly under the Lord, and they think He often changes His moods. They'll say things like, "You never know what God is going to do," and "You can't put God in a box." God is definitely bigger than—and outside of—the little "box" you've tried to contain Him in, but He has also established spiritual laws that even He will not break.

> Thou hast magnified thy word above all thy name.
>
> PSALM 138:2

Although many scriptures reveal the power of the name of Jesus (Phil. 2:9–11), God has magnified His Word even above His name. A person's name is no better than their word. If they don't keep their word, their name isn't accounted for anything. However, the name of Jesus is powerful because He never breaks His Word. When God says something, it becomes a legal, binding contract.

> My covenant will I not break, nor alter the thing that is gone out of my lips.
>
> PSALM 89:34

When God speaks something out of His mouth, His Word is a covenant. It's a contract He will not break.

Jesus upholds "all things by the word of his power" (Heb. 1:3). In other words, our entire universe is held together by the integrity and power of God's Word. If He were to ever break a promise or otherwise violate His Word, this whole world, the universe, and you and I would all self-destruct. It's God's integrity that holds everything together.

The Law of Faith

So when God speaks something out of His mouth, it becomes a contract—a law. Once He's said it, He won't change it. In order to effectively use your authority, you must know what His laws are.

When a new police officer is hired, they immediately study what the laws are that they were hired to enforce. Their police chief doesn't say, "Oh, just go out there without knowing anything and see if it works. Maybe the people will submit." No, that's not their attitude at all. The police officer is thoroughly grilled in what the ordinances and statutes are, what is permissible, and what's not.

Law enforcement officers have to know the law because they can't go beyond it. They can't just do things on their own. A police officer does have authority, but that authority ends at the end of the law. If there isn't a law prescribing what they're trying to enforce, then they can't do it.

It's the same in the spiritual realm. You can't just pick and choose according to your own selfish whims. You must know what the laws are that govern the kingdom of God, and then abide by them. If you try to enforce something outside of those laws, it won't work. You can't just use your God-given authority to do your own thing.

Romans 3 speaks of "the law of faith."

> Where is boasting then? It is excluded. By what law? of works? Nay: but by the law of faith.
>
> ROMANS 3:27

Faith has a law. There is a law of faith.

Law or Phenomenon?

In the physical realm, there are natural laws. Among many others, there is the law of gravity and the law of thrust and lift. A law is something that's both constant and universal. If gravity only operated in the United States and not in some other country, then it would be a phenomenon, but not a law. A law means that it's consistent for everybody on the planet. It's the same for everyone, and it's always that way.

While gravity doesn't just spike every once in a while, occasionally you'll see things that might make you think that. A few years ago, a plane was landing in Colorado Springs. As it was making a turn to come in to land, all of a sudden it accelerated and just dove into the ground. It made a crater, and the largest piece of the plane they could find was one or two foot square. It just exploded and everyone was killed. The investigators did about four years worth of research, but never did find a pilot error or mechanical reason for the crash. However, neither did they say, "Gravity just increased ten times and all of a sudden made that plane crash like that." No, they didn't even consider that a possibility because gravity is a law—it's consistent. They didn't say, "The law of thrust and lift just ceased to operate." No, it's a law—it always operates that way.

If you are ever going to have an efficient, effective, powerful relationship with God, you must break out of this mindset that God is inconsistent. You must get out of this thinking that says, "Sometimes God wills to do this and sometimes He wills to do that. You never know what kind of mood God is in. He might heal this one, but not this other. He may want them to suffer that way the rest of their life." That's not how God is and it isn't the way His kingdom operates.

God is the One who created the heaven and the earth. It's so orderly and systematic that you can go back five years or even five thousand years, and find out exactly where Mars, Jupiter, and all the other planets were. Everything is like clockwork, perfect and consistent. You can accurately project when an eclipse will occur because it's so predictable.

I'm amazed how people can think that God, who created such order in the universe, would do things sporadically and haphazardly in our lives. Order didn't come from chaos. God Himself is orderly. He created laws—both natural and spiritual. God Himself is consistent and predictable because He operates by His own spiritual laws.

You need to find out what His spiritual laws are. Then once you do, take your authority as a believer and enforce these laws. If you're ignorant of God's Word, then you won't be very effective in releasing your authority because Satan will just talk you out of it.

Ignorant of What's Been Provided

Back in the days when people still traveled across the Atlantic by ship, a man scraped together everything he had to buy a ticket to the United States. All he had left was just a tiny little bit of money with which he bought some crackers and cheese. For the entire month-long voyage across the Atlantic, all he had to eat were these crackers and cheese. He watched as all the other passengers feasted sumptuously on the daily bounty of food and drink in the dining room, however he didn't have any money for food, so he just ate a little bit of his crackers and cheese.

Toward the end of the voyage, one of the porters came up to this man and asked, "Sir, I notice that you have never joined us in the dining room. Was there something we've done that offended you? Why didn't you eat with us on this voyage?"

The man answered, "Oh, no. I'm not offended at all. I would have loved to have eaten with you. The food looked so good, but I just didn't have any money left. All I had was enough to buy me some crackers and cheese."

Dumbfounded, the porter looked at this man and said, "But didn't you realize that the meals came with the ticket? They were included in the price that you paid."

This man was ignorant of what was rightfully his, and because of it he did without. All that time the truth was that he could have daily dined sumptuously on anything he wanted of the feasts that were prepared throughout the entire trip.

So many Christians are the same way. They are ignorant of the abundant life God has given us. Consequently, they live without enjoying many of the salvation benefits Jesus died on the cross to provide. Because they are unaware of what the Word says, Satan has them convinced, "You aren't really going to prosper. You'll just have barely enough to get by."

Are you aware of what the Word promises you concerning prosperity? Deuteronomy 28:8 says that God has commanded His blessing upon all the work of your hands. Psalm 35:27 reveals that God delights in the prosperity of His servants. If you don't know these spiritual laws, you won't enforce them. You won't demand Satan to quit stealing from you and to turn loose of your God-given provision. You won't experience what's rightfully yours in Christ. So in order for you to use your authority and experience God's blessings, you need to know what the spiritual laws are and what has been provided for you.

This Confidence We Have

Just yesterday, a mutual friend coerced me to pray for a certain woman with arthritis. I tried to get her to a place of faith by telling her about all the different people I had personally seen healed of arthritis, and that arthritis was no problem for God. She just looked at me and said, "I believe that God can heal, but I don't believe that you can heal." Of course it's God's power and not mine, but He has given me the authority to use it. Not understanding this, she was immediately put off and began resisting how I was trying to minister to her. Then she stated, "It all depends upon whether or not it's God's will to heal me." She believed God could do it, but not that healing is a law—something He's already done.

Through the death, burial, and resurrection of the Lord Jesus Christ, God has already healed every person who will ever be healed. By the stripes Jesus took across His back two thousand years ago, we *were*—past tense—healed. (1 Pet. 2:24.) God isn't healing people right now. He did His part a long time ago. The law was passed, and now healing belongs to us. Still, it's up to us as believers to know what God's will is and command it to come to pass.

> This is the confidence that we have in him, that, if we ask any thing according to his will, he heareth us: and if we know that he hear us, whatsoever we ask, we know that we have the petitions that we desired of him.
>
> 1 JOHN 5:14,15

This confidence that we have, if we ask anything *according to His will,* we know that He hears us, and if we know that He hears us, then *we know we have these petitions.* The whole thing hinges on "What is God's will?"

Some people say, "Well, you never know what God's will is." That kind of thought undermines this whole principle. If you think that

God just sometimes wills for a person to be saved, healed, or prospered, and sometimes doesn't, then you don't know what God's will is. If you think God is totally unpredictable, then you'll never use your authority effectively because you aren't sure what the laws are.

No Exceptions

A police officer can't effectively enforce the law if they think that sometimes it's okay to speed, and other times it's not. Is it okay to rob a bank sometimes, but other times not? Is it permissible to murder occasionally? No, that's not the way the law is. The law isn't sometimes in effect, and other times not. The law is constant—it's the same all the time for everybody.

In the natural realm, we say, "Nobody is above the law." That means that politicians, police officers, whoever it is will be held accountable if they break the law. It doesn't always work out that way, but that's the philosophy we desire to live by.

It's the same in the spiritual realm. There are no exceptions. The Word doesn't just work for some people but not for others. It's not that God just likes some people and causes His power to work for them, but others He doesn't. That's not it at all. God has established laws, and we need to learn how to cooperate with them.

Remember, we can be confident that we will receive anything we ask according to His will. How can we know God's will? God's Word reveals His will.

> Beloved, I wish [will, want, desire] above all things that thou mayest prosper and be in health, even as thy soul prospereth.
>
> 3 JOHN 1:2

God's wish, will, and desire is that you may prosper and be in health, even as your soul (your mind, will, and emotions) prospers.

This is a law of God. He wants you to prosper and be healthy. God wants you to be a world overcomer. (1 John 5:5.)

Good God, Bad Devil

John 10:10 reveals both God's will and Satan's will very clearly.

> The thief cometh not, but for to steal, and to kill, and to destroy: I am come that they might have life, and that they might have it more abundantly.

Satan comes to steal, kill, and destroy, but God comes to give you life more abundantly. If something is life and good, it's God. But if something is bad—stealing, killing, and destroying—it's the devil. Although this is a bit simplistic, it's true. Good God. Bad devil. Good things come from God and bad things come from the devil. (James 1:17.)

The Lord has ordained laws for your good, so you can access the abundant life He's provided for you. Nevertheless, you must learn what these laws are so you can cooperate with them and demand Satan to quit stealing, killing, and destroying the blessings that are rightfully yours.

In the natural realm, if someone stole something of yours, you have the right to press charges. You could demand for that person to be picked up by the police and prosecuted. If they're found guilty, some kind of punishment or prison, retribution or reimbursement could be assessed. Yet, it's all dependent upon the person who was wronged exercising their rights and pressing charges. In a sense, you have to take your authority and say, "I'm going to receive what's rightfully mine."

It's the same in the spiritual realm. Just like every other believer, you have God-given rights and privileges. He has established His will for us, but it's up to you to claim what God has done for you. You must press the issue. You have to take your authority and enforce those spiritual laws that have been made for your benefit. Ignorance of the spiritual laws will keep you from pressing charges. It will prevent you from keeping Satan out of the picture. The devil just runs wild when you think you don't have any authority or power.

Many Christians just don't know what is rightfully theirs. Thinking they have to be sick, poor, and discouraged, they say, "This is just the way that it is. I can't do anything about it." They don't know that Jesus Christ has redeemed us from these things.

Constant and Universal

In the same way that the physical world operates under natural laws, God has created His kingdom to operate under spiritual laws. These laws are constant and universal, so it's to your benefit to learn what they are and then cooperate with them.

You can't just pick and choose, saying, "Since I have authority as a believer, I'm going to command that I get this house or that car. It's under my power and authority, so I command it and say it's so." No, you have to cooperate with the laws of God. As a matter of fact, there are laws of God that specifically tell you not to covet your neighbor's house, car, or wife. God doesn't have a law that promises you can use His power for selfish purposes to claim, "This person will die so I can marry their mate." That's not going to work because the Lord hasn't provided it for you. There aren't any spiritual laws in the kingdom of God that work selfishly.

CHAPTER 19

How the Power Flows

The woman who had an issue of blood powerfully illustrates these truths about how the kingdom of God operates by law.

> A certain woman, which had an issue of blood twelve years, and had suffered many things of many physicians, and had spent all that she had, and was nothing bettered, but rather grew worse, when she had heard of Jesus, came in the press behind, and touched his garment. For she said, If I may touch but his clothes, I shall be whole. And straightway the fountain of her blood was dried up; and she felt in her body that she was healed of that plague.
>
> And Jesus, immediately knowing in himself that virtue had gone out of him, turned him about in the press, and said, Who touched my clothes? And his disciples said unto him, Thou seest the multitude thronging thee, and sayest thou, Who touched me? And he looked round about to see her that had done this thing. But the woman fearing and trembling, knowing what was done in her, came and fell down before him, and told him all the truth. And he said unto her, Daughter, thy faith hath made thee whole; go in peace, and be whole of thy plague.
>
> MARK 5:25–34

Jesus was in the midst of a multitude of people who were thronging Him. That means they were crowding in close, constantly bumping into and touching Him. Many people were reaching out, touching Him, and trying to receive their healing. Yet, this little woman with the issue of blood came, touched the hem of His garment, and instantly the power of God flowed right through Jesus' body, through His garment, and into this woman. Immediately, she was healed of an infirmity that had plagued her for twelve long years. As soon as this happened, Jesus turned around and asked, "Who touched Me?"

Jesus Increased

Some people believe this religious concept that Jesus knew all things. Therefore, they consider this question to be purely rhetorical, saying, "Jesus didn't really mean it. He already knew everything that had to go on." I don't think that's not accurate at all. The Word says that...

> Jesus increased in wisdom and stature, and in favour with God and man.
>
> LUKE 2:52

Jesus was fully God, but He was also fully man. Because He was in the flesh—a physical, human body—He had to learn things the same way that you and I do. The Word here says that He increased in wisdom and knowledge.

In His spirit, Jesus was Lord at His birth. That's what the angels said when they made their announcement to the shepherds.

> For unto you is born this day in the city of David a Saviour, which is Christ the Lord.
>
> LUKE 2:11

Even though in His spirit realm He was God, Jesus didn't come out of the womb speaking Hebrew. He had to learn to eat, walk, and talk. He had to learn who He was. Because Jesus was in a physical body, He had to deal with limitations—not limitations from sin, but limitations due to the fact that God didn't make our physical part able to perceive things that we haven't yet learned through our senses. So when Jesus was walking through this crowd and this woman touched Him, He perceived the power of God flowing out of Him, but He didn't know who had touched Him.

"Who Touched Me?"

Most people think that when you approach God for healing (or anything else) that He evaluates you to see if you're worthy. They think that once you make your petition, God measures how worthy you are—whether you've been good enough, moral enough, paid your tithes, fasted long enough, have enough other people praying for you, and if your situation is desperate enough. Then, based on His personal evaluation, He either releases His power and you get healed, or He retains His power and says, "Nope, you haven't prayed enough, you aren't holy enough, you haven't fasted enough, and/or you have this sin in your life and until you deal with it I won't heal you." People tend to view God this way, that He's up there in heaven evaluating us and then, depending on His evaluation, He either releases His power or not.

These verses in Mark 5 completely kill this misconception. Jesus didn't know who this woman was. He didn't see her coming. She touched the hem of His garment. He perceived the outflow of power, but then asked, "Who touched Me?" Jesus honestly didn't know who had touched Him. Therefore, He didn't evaluate her to see if she was worthy or not. This shows that the power of God flows under law.

When you tap into these spiritual laws, the power of God just flows. The Lord doesn't size up one person, saying, "You're worthy. I'm going to release My power to you," and then looks over another, saying, "No, you aren't worthy." It's not like that at all. There are just laws that govern how the power of God works. When you cooperate with those laws and put them into effect, the power flows. If you don't, the power doesn't flow. It's nothing about God loving one person more than another. It's just a matter of law. God established His kingdom to operate under spiritual laws. As believers, we need to find out what those laws are and cooperate with them.

Electricity operates under law. If you're grounded and you grab a live wire, it'll kill you. It's not that the electric company looked at you and said, "Let's teach them a lesson." No, there are just natural laws. You put those laws into effect, and so the power flowed.

On the other hand, a bird can land on a high wire and not be electrocuted because they aren't grounded. It's not because the electric company loves birds more than they love people. There are just laws that govern how this power flows.

Electricity has been around since God created the earth. It's always been here in the form of thunderstorms and static electricity. People could have used electricity thousands of years ago if they would have understood the laws that governed it. God didn't just "create" electricity a few hundred years ago, and "allowed" people to start using it. No, electricity always was available to be harnessed for our use. Our ignorance of those laws kept us from being benefited by it.

God Didn't Shut Off the Power

It's the same in the spiritual realm. It wasn't God who let healing, the gifts of the Holy Spirit, and other supernatural aspects of our faith just "pass away" for more than a thousand years. That's not what happened. God didn't shut off the power. People entered the Dark Ages because they didn't retain the knowledge of the things of God.

The early New Testament church operated strongly in the power of God. Then years later and for whatever reason, the church at large came to this place of believing that God's miracles and supernatural power passed away with the apostles. Then, in the early 1900s, the power of the Holy Spirit began to manifest again in places like Azusa Street. There was an influx of healings, deliverance, speaking in tongues, and miracles that have continued to snowball worldwide up until this present day.

It wasn't God who turned the power off after the first 200 years of Christianity and then turned it back on again 1,700 years later. It's not that He operates in cycles, and now we're in a "wave" or a "move" of God. That's not how it works any more than it was God who kept people from using electricity, airplanes, and cars a thousand years ago. All the laws were here, but people's ignorance kept them from taking advantage of these laws. Due to their ignorance, people died of heat when they could have had air conditioning if they had known what the laws were. People were hindered from moving over long distances in a short period of time. They had to walk, or ride a camel, donkey, or horse. It wasn't God that kept them in ignorance. They just didn't know these things.

It's not God who isn't healing or blessing you. It's not the Lord who has "willed" that you suffer. God has created laws, but you need to discover what they are. As you learn how to cooperate with and enforce these laws, you'll see God's provision for you manifest.

You might be thinking, *I disagree. That puts all the responsibility on me. You're saying that it's up to me to take hold of what God has provided.*

Yes, that's exactly what I'm saying. It's not God who hasn't healed, prospered, or delivered you. It's our own ignorance that keeps us in these bondages. God has already done His part. The Word clearly reveals that the Lord has already healed us, but we have yet to take advantage of it. (1 Pet. 2:24.)

Unbelief Hinders Receiving

Let's go back to Mark 5 and continue looking at this woman who touched the hem of Jesus' garment. Verse 31 says that there was a multitude of people thronging Him. This could have been as many as three or four hundred people trying to follow Jesus through these city streets. However many it was, there were a lot of people pressing Him. They didn't just want to be near Him, they wanted to draw near because there had been power and virtue flowing out of Him and healing people. A multitude of people were there, of which many needed to be healed and delivered. Yet, only one person out of the many received healing.

This wasn't the only time this happened. The same thing happened in John 5 at the pool of Bethesda. There was a multitude of impotent folk, yet one person received healing. Why is it that one person gets healed when there are many who need it?

Maybe you haven't received your healing. You know of other people who have. Why haven't you been healed? One reason could be that you don't understand that God has already done His part. You aren't taking your authority and enforcing spiritual laws. You're ignorant of what God has already said and done, so you're passively going to Him asking, "God, will You please heal me, if it be Your will? Lord, will You set me free and move in my life?" You can say that many different ways, but the Bible calls it "unbelief." If you are asking God to do those things, then you aren't believing the record.

When God said, "By whose stripes ye were healed" (1 Pet. 2:24), He put your healing into the past tense as an already accomplished reality. He's already done it. Therefore, you ought to believe the Word and say, "I know it's already done. He put the same power on the inside of me that raised Jesus from the dead. (Eph. 1:18–20.) I take my authority and now I speak to my problem and command these things to happen." But instead of taking your authority, you're just going passively to God and saying, "God, will You please heal me, if it be Your will?" That's unbelief, and if that's what you are doing, it's the reason you aren't receiving. You're ignorant of God's spiritual laws.

Words

This woman with the issue of blood said:

> If I may touch but his clothes, I shall be whole.
>
> MARK 5:28

Although there are many different spiritual laws, one of them that governs whether you receive from God or not is the power of your words.

> A man's belly shall be satisfied with the fruit of his mouth; and with the increase of his lips shall he be filled. Death and life are in the power of the tongue: and they that love it shall eat the fruit thereof.
>
> PROVERBS 18:20,21

Although many different scriptures reveal the importance of our words (see Matt. 12:34–37; James 3; Mark 11), this verse clearly reveals that both death and life are in the power of the tongue.

When we're trying to receive a healing from the Lord, many of us ignore this law and say, "I've heard people talk about this name it and claim it, blab it and grab it group who tell people they can have what they say. They say you're supposed to say you're healed when you don't feel healed. Well, I just don't believe in that stuff." So when somebody asks, "How are you?" the person they ask says, "Well, I'm dying. I only have a week to live. The doctor told me it's terrible. I feel so bad." This individual is releasing death with their mouth through their negative speech. Yet, they'll go to the Lord in "prayer" and say, "Oh, God. Heal me, if it be Your will." Then when they don't see a physical healing manifest, they get upset with God as if He failed. There are laws that govern how to receive healing. One of them is you will have what you say. (Mark 11:23.)

You can't speak death out of your mouth and expect to receive life. It doesn't work that way. You might say, "I just don't believe that." Fine. That's just like a person saying, "I just don't believe that copper is a better conductor of electricity than wood. I'm going to wire my house with wood, not copper." When they plug the electricity into the connection of wood, I guarantee the power isn't going to flow. It won't run your lights, appliances, or air conditioning. You may not like this, but it's how God established these laws.

Wood or Copper?

Faith flows through words. Words release either death or life, but your ignorance of this law doesn't mean that the law is going to change. You can declare, "I can say whatever I want to and it doesn't make any difference." That's not true. It's not how the spiritual laws of the kingdom operate any more than wood is a better conductor of electricity than copper. It's not up to you to make the laws. You just need to discover what they are and then enforce them. God's Word says that faith speaks. (Rom. 10:6.)

This woman in Mark 5 started putting some of the spiritual laws of God into effect when she said, "If I may but touch the hem of His garment, I shall be made whole." When she did, the power of God began to flow. Jesus didn't size her up and evaluate her worthiness. God's power flows when we cooperate with the spiritual laws of His kingdom. Electricity isn't personal when it kills someone. There are just laws at work governing the flow of power. Either you can cooperate and use electricity to your advantage, or those same laws will kill you.

It's the same way in the kingdom of God. There are many people who pray for healing because they don't understand the spiritual laws that govern it. When they don't see healing manifest, they get mad at God saying, "Lord, if You wanted to, You could have healed this person." No, God has set up the kingdom to operate under laws, and He can't just violate them.

The Lord doesn't want people to die from gravity—falling off bridges, buildings, or cliffs. That's not God's will. However, a Colorado Springs man was climbing on some rocks on a mountain nearby and he fell about three hundred feet. He was one of our soldiers who survived Iraq, but he didn't survive this fall. It wasn't God's will for this man to die, but what's the Lord going to do? Will He stop the law of gravity to save this man's life? Although God is the One who created the laws that govern this physical world, if He were to suspend gravity because He didn't want this guy to die, there would have been multitudes of other people depending on the law of gravity who would have died.

God created these laws, and He doesn't just suspend them. If you don't cooperate with the law of gravity, you could get killed. If you jump off a ten-story building, gravity will kill you. God intended gravity to be to your advantage and to help you function here on this earth. If you're sitting in a chair right now, you don't have to force yourself to stay down. Gravity is working. The same law that will help you if you cooperate with it, will also kill you if you violate it. It's the same way in the spiritual realm.

CHAPTER 20

Cooperate With God

Some people don't like these truths at all. It's comforting to them to feel that God is the One who willed for this person to die and that one to fail, this person to have a nervous breakdown and that marriage to break up. They find comfort in this mentality because it takes all responsibility away from them and they're able to say, "Whatever will be, will be." I understand that these truths I'm sharing will unsettle some people, but it's the truth that will set them free. (John 8:32.)

Before my wife and I were married, there was a girl we were both very close friends with. I was with her when she died. She was praying and saying, "God's going to heal me. Now is the time. It has to be now." She was believing for healing. We were shocked when she died because we honestly expected God to heal her. Although it took me almost four years to learn enough of God's Word to figure out what had happened, I finally realized that we had violated many spiritual laws and done many things wrong.

God's Messenger Boy?

At that time in my life, I was under the false teaching that says, "God puts tragedy in your life to perfect you. He'll bless you with sickness and disease because it's through your hardships that you are made better." This is absolutely untrue, but back then I didn't understand enough of the Word to know any better. So I believed it, and accepted it.

I actually attended an out-of-state conference where I heard a man teach that Satan was God's messenger boy. He said, "Anything the devil wants to do in your life, he has to get God's permission. Ultimately, God is the One who's controlling both the good and the bad, so bad things are actually sent from God to perfect us." When I returned home from this conference, I gave a tape of this message entitled, "Satan Is God's Messenger Boy," to my friend. She immediately listened to it.

In the message, this man used the example of a high school boy who was too timid and shy to witness. Even though he wasn't bold enough to speak to others about his faith, he wanted the Lord to use him, so he said, "God, I'll do anything. Put sickness or disease on me so that people will see that I'm not afraid to die."

The very next day, this boy came down with leukemia and eventually died of it. While sick and dying, he witnessed to people. Since he was a football player, the whole school turned out at his funeral. At the ceremony, four people were born again.

This man used that as an example of how God answered this boy's prayer to be a witness by "blessing" him with leukemia. This girl listened to that tape and prayed the exact same prayer as that boy. "God, give me leukemia so I can be a witness." The next day, she passed out. They rushed her to the hospital. She had acute leukemia, and eventually died of it.

God wasn't the One who answered that prayer. He doesn't put sickness and disease on us. Satan is the one who takes advantage of a "prayer" like that. Both of those young people dropped all their defenses and opened themselves up to leukemia believing it was of God.

Double-Minded

When this girl died, four people were born again at her funeral. I was there. I saw it. Some people thought, *It must not have been God's will to heal her.* How dumb can you get and still breathe? I'm not saying this to be critical of anyone. I was personally involved in this situation. We were so stupid that we were asking God for cancer.

If you start asking God for cancer, believing He is a source of it, it will come your way. It's not that God sent it, but there are lying spirits that masquerade themselves as angels of light who will claim to be His messenger. (2 Cor. 11:14.) If you start praying for tragedy in your life, you'll get plenty of it—and you'll think it's from God.

There are laws that govern how God operates. We asked for this sickness and submitted to it, claiming it was the Lord. Because of that, we never fought against it. We never actively resisted the devil because—in our warped way of thinking—that would have been fighting against God. We thought He was the One who gave this sickness. So there we were asking for sickness, believing God answered our prayer by giving this girl leukemia, and then, on the other hand, asking Him to take it away. That's double-minded.

> Let not that [double-minded] man think that he shall receive any thing of the Lord.
>
> JAMES 1:7

That's violating and voiding the laws of God.

This girl died through my influence. I had a part in it. Some people don't want to accept responsibility. Maybe you know someone who died. Perhaps you've lost a marriage because you didn't understand the laws of God. You didn't know how to stand and fight. Those tragedies and negative things you've experienced weren't God's will—it was your fault, or the devil, or someone else. Many people don't want to accept this responsibility. They'd rather blame God. I understand how you feel because I've been there. Yet, I accepted responsibility. I realized that we did so many things wrong. We violated God's Word and opened up a door for the devil through false teaching and wrong believing.

I accepted my responsibility, and I've changed. I've believed the truth, and the truth has set me free. Since then, I've seen many people healed of leukemia. I can't undo what's done, but I can redeem that situation by going and sharing these truths with other people and seeing them set free.

Jesus Couldn't?

In Mark 6, Jesus went into His own hometown.

> When the sabbath day was come, he began to teach in the synagogue: and many hearing him were astonished, saying, From whence hath this man these things? and what wisdom is this which is given unto him, that even such mighty works are wrought by his hands? Is not this the carpenter, the son of Mary, the brother of James, and Joses, and of Judah, and Simon? and are not his sisters here with us? And they were offended at him.
>
> MARK 6:2,3

These people knew Jesus as the carpenter, the son of Joseph and Mary. However, the truth is that He wasn't a carpenter or Joseph's son. Jesus was the Son of God who happened to work as a carpenter for a period of time. These people knew Him in the physical, natural realm, but they didn't know who He truly was. Due to this, they rejected His ministry thinking, *He's making Himself out to be somebody better than us. He grew up here with my kids. I've seen Him since He was a tiny little boy, and here He is proclaiming that He's the Son of God.* Because of their familiarity with Jesus, they were offended at Him and rejected Him.

> But Jesus, said unto them, A prophet is not without honour, but in his own country, and among his own kin, and in his own house. And he could there do no mighty work, save that he laid his hands upon a few sick folk, and healed them.
>
> MARK 6:4,5

Notice how Jesus *could* do no mighty work there. It's not that He wouldn't do it—He couldn't.

When many people pray and ask for something and it doesn't come to pass, they think it was God that chose not to do it. God is not free to move independent of us. He has to have a believer—knowing what the laws are and taking their authority—to flow through. We must cooperate with God. If you pray and don't see something come to pass, you need to evaluate: Have you cooperated with God's laws? Is what you prayed for something He's promised? If you're praying for something that isn't revealed in the Word—stop. It's not good for you and God hasn't provided it.

When something, like healing, is promised to you in the Word, take your place of authority as a believer and say, "This is a law of God, so I command my body to respond. In the name of Jesus, I am commanding what God has already done to manifest." But you have to know what has been promised.

Mark 6:5 says that Jesus *could* do no mighty work. It's not that He wouldn't do it, He couldn't do it. God Himself will not violate our free will. He won't make you receive. He has provided—generated—the power, but you must cooperate and flip the switch. You must learn how to receive what God has already done.

Your Free Will

It isn't the Lord who is letting people die and go to hell. People are choosing to go to hell because God gave them a free choice. Regardless, He's doing everything He can to keep that from coming to pass.

No one who is condemned to hell on Judgment Day will be able to put their finger in Jesus' face and say, "It's not fair. You didn't give me a chance!" God has put obstacles and barriers in front of every person who is headed to hell. They've had to climb over their own conscience that has convicted them and told them they were wrong and should repent. God used other people to be a witness to them in some way during their lifetime. There has been obstacle after obstacle. God is faithful to deal with every person who has ever lived, trying to turn them from their destructive ways. But they choose to reject His drawing and ignore Him, so no one will be able to accuse God. He's not the one sending people to hell. They'll know that it was absolutely their choice.

It's the same with healing. It's not God who is letting people be sick. He's already provided for the healing of every single person. The problem is we're ignorant of His provision and His laws governing how to receive it.

Just as Jesus could do no mighty work in His own hometown because of the unbelief of the people there, unbelief prevents God from doing what He wants to do in people's lives today. (Matt. 13:58.) It wasn't Christ's unbelief or lack of willingness, but their unbelief that hindered His power. Our unbelief stops God from doing His will.

God will not move in your life without your cooperation. You must be in agreement with Him. That's one of His laws. Your free will is something that the Lord will not violate. You may desire the right end results, but you won't receive them if you disobey every single law along the way. You may wish to enjoy good health, but if you're committing sexual immorality shacking up with anybody and everybody, through those actions you are putting a law into effect, the law of sowing and reaping (Gal. 6:7–8), and faith for good health is dead without accompanying works (James 2:17). You can't just pray for something, and then act in a contrary way. That's not how the kingdom works.

Powerful and Important

I recently prayed with a woman in a hospital. She was very close to death and looked terrible. Since she was barely alive, she couldn't talk or communicate. I tried everything I knew to discern if there was anything I could minister to her or her family, but I couldn't perceive anything, so I just prayed for her the best I knew how and left.

Right before I left town, the family called and told me that she was going downhill fast. The doctor only gave her an hour or two to live. Since I was busy holding a meeting, I sent some friends back to the hospital. After she passed on, my friends were talking to the family. They discovered that this woman had said, "I give up. I'm ready to die." She had quit believing. I was trying to exercise my authority and minister healing, but it was against this woman's will. It doesn't work that way.

God gave us a free choice. Even a medical doctor will tell you that once someone loses the will to live, they'll die. The ailment could even be something minor that could be treated by medicine, but without that will to live, they'll die. However, when some people go beyond medicine's ability to help and the doctors say, "There is nothing we can do for them; they're going to die," some people just have a will to live and they fight through. Your personal will is very powerful and important.

One of God's laws is that you can't have your will in one direction and then expect to get the results that would come from going in another. You can't just yield to and serve the devil, giving him total access to you, and reap the benefits of a godly life. It's not because God won't flow, or that He's looking at you as being unworthy. We're all unworthy in that sense. God doesn't move in our lives because we deserve it. However, in order to see His provision—His will—manifest, you do have to cooperate with Him.

CHAPTER 21

As You Think

You need to learn what God's laws are and then cooperate with them. You can't watch television programs that minister depression and then operate in joy. You can't take in all of the (bad) news without strengthening unbelief. If you want a pure heart, you can't watch movies that are full of adultery and fornication. You're going to have to think on things that are true, honest, just, pure, lovely, virtuous, praiseworthy, and of good report. (Phil. 4:8.) Yet people misunderstand these laws.

Your life moves in the direction of your dominant thoughts.

> As he thinketh in his heart, so is he.
>
> PROVERBS 23:7

You will reap emotions based on those things on which you focus your attention.

> For to be carnally minded is death; but to be spiritually minded is life and peace.
>
> ROMANS 8:6

That's a law of God. The fact is you can't experience God's peace if you're constantly meditating on things that are contrary to peace—hatred, strife, and ungodliness. You can't just pray and ask for peace. You must learn to keep your thoughts centered on God and His Word.

> Thou wilt keep him in perfect peace, whose mind is stayed on thee: because he trusteth in thee.
>
> ISAIAH 26:3

The Knowledge of God

Your emotions will follow what you think. That's a law of God. So if you're praying for peace but aren't focused on God, you're just spitting in the wind. It's not going to work. Desiring the things of God is part of the process, but it's not all there is to it.

> Grace and peace be multiplied unto you through the knowledge of God, and of Jesus our Lord.
>
> 2 PETER 1:2

Grace and peace are multiplied to you through the knowledge of God and of Jesus Christ our Lord—not through prayer. It isn't a matter of you just pleading with God. The laws of God say that you must think on the right things to receive the right results.

> Rejoice in the Lord always: and again I say, Rejoice. Let your moderation be known unto all men. The Lord is at hand. Be careful [full of care] for nothing; but in every thing by prayer and supplication with thanksgiving let your requests be made known unto God. And the peace of God, which passeth all understanding, shall keep your hearts and minds through Christ Jesus.
>
> PHILIPPIANS 4:4–7

As you keep your mind stayed upon the Lord, the peace of God will keep your heart and mind. The next verse continues about our thoughts, saying:

> Finally, brethren, whatsoever things are true, whatsoever things are honest, whatsoever things are just, whatsoever things are pure, whatsoever things are lovely, whatsoever things are of good report; if there be any virtue, and if there be any praise, *think on these things.*
>
> PHILIPPIANS 4:8

In other words, this is a command to keep your mind stayed on the Lord and His Word. (Isa. 26:3.)

These are laws of God. This is how His kingdom works.

The Gos-pill

God made you so that your physical and emotional health follows the way you think. If you're thinking on depressing things, you'll be depressed. If you're thinking on the Lord and His Word, you'll be full of life, joy, and peace.

God's Word is…

> Life unto those that find them, and health to all their flesh.
>
> PROVERBS 4:22

The Word of God brings health.

> He sent his word, and healed them, and delivered them from their destructions.
>
> PSALM 107:20

God's prescription for health is His Word. Take it in daily doses, just like medicine. Many people are praying for health, but they're violating the Great Physician's instructions. They aren't taking their medicine.

What if the medical doctor you saw about your condition prescribed to you a method of treatment—taking a certain pill each day—yet you didn't take them. Then, you get upset at the doctor about your treatment, saying, "It's no good. It didn't work." Actually, since you didn't take the pills, you have no right to criticize the doctor. You didn't cooperate with the prescribed treatment. The medical doctor gave you a treatment, but you didn't follow it.

God has given us a treatment. He's prescribed to us the Gos-pill (Gospel). He sent His Word to heal us and deliver us from all our destructions. (Ps. 107:20.) God's Word is health to all our flesh and life to those who find it. (Prov. 4:22.) This is the Great Physician's prescription.

Exceeding Abundantly Above

In the kingdom of God, there are laws governing faith and healing. Yet, we continue to violate these laws. Then we pray for healing and wonder why we aren't receiving. That's ignorance gone to seed!

Please don't take this as condemnation. I'm not trying to condemn anyone. I just want to stop people from condemning God. They say, "It's God's will that so and so died, this business didn't work, that marriage broke up, my children are rebellious," and on and on they go. Why do they put the blame on God? Many have the mindset, "Because I prayed and asked for something and it didn't come to pass." They just totally ignore the fact that God can't do everything He wants to do. There are laws that govern how His kingdom operates. If we violate those laws, we're actually empowering the devil to come in and steal, kill, and destroy. We need to cooperate with God's laws to receive His abundant life.

Most people think that God is able to do exceeding abundantly above all that we ask or think, but that's not true. You must read the entire verse to get the true meaning.

> Now unto him that is able to do exceeding abundantly above all that we ask or think, *according to the power that worketh in us.*
>
> EPHESIANS 3:20

That last phrase puts a limitation on the first one. God isn't free to move in your life independent of you. He has set it up to where He has to flow through people. He doesn't control your life without your consent or agreement. There has to be power working on the inside of you—specifically the power of faith. You have to stir yourself up and make that faith come alive.

Many people just plop themselves down in front of the television. They become discouraged and depressed listening to all of the bad news. They spend virtually no time with God and no time in His Word. Then they just throw a prayer out, and if it doesn't come to pass, "Well then, God failed."

It is absolutely wrong for us to condemn God. It isn't God who is failing to be good, or failing to answer people's prayers. It's us who fail to understand how to receive. We don't realize that there are laws that govern even God's operation. He's not going to resist the devil for you. God isn't going to do what He told you to do. (James 4:7.) He commanded you to go heal the sick. (Matt. 10:8.) He generated the power and placed it on the inside of you—the very same power that raised Christ from the dead. (Eph. 1:18–20.) He equipped you, but then He told you to go lay hands on the sick, and they would recover. (Mark 16:18.)

Many of us are violating every instruction and admonition in the Word of God and then throwing a prayer out. If it doesn't work, then God failed. That's not true. God is faithful, faithful, faithful!

I'm the Problem—Not God

I've had bad things happen in my life. People who were close to me died—even after I prayed for their healing. However, in most of these cases, I can see that I am the one who missed it. In some situations, I still don't understand exactly why things worked out the way that they have, but I've come to this firm conviction that God is always faithful. He never fails. If bad things happen somehow, I failed to understand and cooperate with the laws of God.

I find comfort in knowing that I'm the problem—not God. This is one of the great benefits in understanding the authority of the believer. Yet most people are just the opposite. They can't handle taking responsibility for failure in their lives. Yes, this understanding puts responsibility on us, but it also explains why we don't always see things work. God doesn't always have people who will cooperate with His laws.

The release of God's power in your life is directly proportional to how you believe. It's not proportional to your holiness. All of us fail and come short in different ways. The issue is faith. You get what you believe. If you believe that God has already healed you and you begin to exercise your authority, you'll see that healing manifest. But if you believe God can heal but He hasn't done it yet, then that healing won't come to pass. Just because you don't like how the kingdom works, doesn't mean that it changes the laws. This is just how God is.

CHAPTER 22

Honor God

When you cooperate with God's spiritual laws, His power flows. When you disobey them, it stops the power of God from operating. We see this very clearly in Mark 5 in the account of the woman with the issue of blood.

> A certain woman, which had an issue of blood twelve years, and had suffered many things of many physicians, and had spent all that she had, and was nothing bettered, but rather grew worse.
>
> MARK 5:25,26

This lady had gone to physicians for twelve years. Although their treatments had depleted every penny she had, they hadn't helped her a bit.

Doctors Aren't Infallible

If a woman like this were to come to me seeking healing and give me every penny she had yet still not be healed, someone would be on the news accusing me of being a crook and a charlatan. Since we just expect the power of God to always work instantly, they would come against a preacher. However, we don't have any second thoughts about giving all of our money—hundreds of thousands of dollars—

to medical doctors who have been known to make mistakes and even kill people. I'm not against doctors. I'm just saying that they aren't infallible. Still, hardly anyone ever considers this fact.

In the natural realm, people understand that there are laws and sometimes problems arise and not everything works out the way it's expected. Yet when it comes to the things of God, people just expect them to work with ease, completely problem free. They don't realize that there are spiritual laws that govern the kingdom of God. It's not that the Lord has a hard time doing things—it's us. We are dealing with things. So there may be a problem in you receiving through me—not because God is a problem, but because I don't know everything and you don't either.

Sometimes when I'm praying with someone, we'll see 50 percent of their healing manifest. So I'll go back and keep praying with them. Other people have come up and asked me, "If it's really God, why do you have to pray for them again and again, standing and believing? If it's God, then they'd just be healed." That's someone who doesn't understand that there are spiritual laws and we're just barely beginning to scratch the surface of understanding how things work. It can take time, not because God has problems, but because I'm having a problem or the person receiving is having a problem. None of us understand everything yet.

The woman with the issue of blood had suffered many years from physicians and their treatments, yet nobody thought anything about it. I'm sure her friends believed she was doing the right thing. As these doctors bled her of everything she had financially without helping her one bit, they'd encourage her to go back to them and try again. No doubt these same friends called her "fanatical" and "extreme" once she had heard of Jesus and decided to pursue receiving her healing supernaturally through Him.

Faith Comes by Hearing

This woman was determined. "She had heard of Jesus" (Mark 5:27), and what He had done for others, which brings us to another law of God. You cannot believe and receive from God without somehow first hearing of Jesus and His Word.

> How then shall they call on him in whom they have not believed? and how shall they believe in him of whom they have not heard?...So then faith cometh by hearing, and hearing by the word of God.
>
> ROMANS 10:14,17

Many people who are trying to believe and receive from God aren't getting into His Word. Faith comes through the Word of God. If you want to increase and release your faith, you need to increase your revelation knowledge of God's Word. That's how simple it is, but there are people who violate this law all the time. They're just expecting to get what they've asked for because they're in a desperate situation. They don't know the first thing about believing God. They don't study the Word. They just sit in front of the television watching all kinds of junk, wondering why their faith isn't increasing.

Both faith and unbelief come by hearing. If you listen to all of the negativity that's on television and radio instead of seeking God, you'll be full of unbelief and you won't receive. That's just a law of God. (See Matt. 6:33.) Some people don't like that and say, "That just doesn't fit my lifestyle." Maybe you ought to change your lifestyle to fit the Word.

I'm amazed at some of the people who come to me wanting God to intervene in their lives. Just in talking to them, it's obvious they haven't spent an hour in the Word in a year. They don't pray or seek God. They haven't been attending church, studying the Word, or listening to Bible teachings. They're living their lives totally for themselves, bound by the discouragement and despair that comes from keeping their mind on evil things. Yet, they want all of the benefits that come from keeping their mind stayed on God. I get upset when people criticize and slander God as if He's the One who failed. The Lord isn't failing. We're the ones who have failed to understand and cooperate with His laws.

Speak and Act

This woman in Mark 5 was committed that she was going to receive something from God.

> For she said, If I may touch but his clothes, I shall be whole.
>
> MARK 5:28

She spoke her faith, and then acted on it. That's one of the laws of God. If she would have stayed on the edge of the crowd, saying, "I believe, I receive; I believe, I receive" without acting on this belief, she would not have received.

In order to act on her faith, she had to overcome what other people thought. That's another spiritual law. Jesus said:

> How can ye believe, which receive honour one of another, and seek not the honour that cometh from God only?
>
> JOHN 5:44

In other words, being a "man-pleaser" will hinder your faith. It'll keep you from believing. Jesus said, "You can't believe if you are seeking the honor that comes from other people instead of from God." If you're worried about what everybody else is going to say, it'll stop you from receiving.

Focus on the Lord

According to Old Testament law, the Jews considered anyone with an issue of blood to be unclean. (Lev. 15:19–33.) If someone touched something that an unclean person had touched such as a saddle, bowl, basin, or clothes, they also became unclean. So anyone who touched an unclean person also became unclean. Due to this, the Jews required an unclean person to stand on the edge of a crowd and yell out "Unclean, unclean," so that people would stay away from them.

When this woman crawled through the crowd and touched the hem of Jesus' garment, she touched people. She could have suffered the wrath of these people, been condemned, and stoned to death. When Jesus pointed her out in front of all these folks, it took a lot of courage for her to come forward.

This woman came to a place where she didn't care what anybody else said. She disdained the personal risk involved in coming to Jesus. She became more focused on the Lord and what He had to say than what these other folks had to say. Many people don't receive from God because they're "man-pleasers."

> The fear of man bringeth a snare.
>
> PROVERBS 29:25

That's a law of God. If you are afraid of other people and what they're going to say, it'll hinder your faith. It'll keep you from receiving what you're believing for. You must come to the place in your heart where you say:

> Let God be true, but every man a liar.
>
> ROMANS 3:4

You must come to the place where you can honestly declare, "God, You are all I care about. I'm going to do what you tell me regardless of the flack that I receive for it." You must believe with all your heart. You can't harbor reservations and fears.

A God-Pleaser Alone

I ministered to a woman once who was sent home from the doctors to die. She had three large cancerous tumors that were open and spurting blood. After prayer, they shrunk to the size of quarters and were easily removed by the doctor as an outpatient procedure.

Although the cancer was miraculously healed by the Lord without the doctors, once they saw the results, they wanted this woman to have radiation treatments just in case there was any cancer remaining. I told her not to do it. God had healed her and not the doctors. She didn't need to expose herself to all the problems that radiation treatments would bring. But she chose to go ahead with the doctors and nearly died from the complications.

After that, once again, I encouraged her that well people don't get radiation treatments and that they weren't necessary. But this woman was worried about what her mother, husband, children, and church people had to say. She knew the Lord had completely healed her and she didn't need any further medical care, but she just couldn't bring herself to go against what these other people said. So she went in for the next round of treatments and died as a direct result of the radiation.

Fearing what other people think brings a snare. (Prov. 29:25.) This is a law of God. You can't truly believe if you are worried about what other people think. (John 5:44.) You must be a God-pleaser alone.

These are just a few of the laws that govern the kingdom of God. As believers exercising our authority, we don't just pick and choose and make God do certain things. All we do is enforce the laws He's already set in place. We discover what God has already provided and how He said it works, and then we cooperate with and enforce those laws.

CHAPTER 23

No New Testament Model

Satan isn't using a superhuman, angelic power and authority. He's using mankind's God-given power and authority that we yielded to him when we obeyed him and disobeyed God. So it's actually nothing but a human power and authority that is being used against us. Therefore, the devil can't do anything against us without our consent and cooperation.

Understanding these truths radically changes our view of spiritual warfare. We recognize that the devil is a defeated foe. Jesus completely stripped him of all power and authority through the cross. However, the warfare we face today is in enforcing the Lord's victory. It's fighting against the wiles of the devil—his deception, lies, trickery, cunningness, and craftiness. (Eph. 6:11.)

All the warfare scriptures in the New Testament reveal that the battle is in our mind.

> For though we walk in the flesh, we do not war after the flesh: (For the weapons of our warfare are not carnal, but mighty through God to the pulling down of strong holds;) Casting down imaginations, and every high thing that exalteth itself against the knowledge

> of God, and bringing into captivity every thought to the obedience of Christ.
>
> 2 CORINTHIANS 10:3–5

Notice what these weapons accomplish: They cast down strongholds, imaginations, every high thing that exalts itself against the knowledge of God, and bring every thought captive. All of this has to do with your thinking. The battlefield is your mind. Satan is fighting us with thoughts, and we counter him with the thoughts God gives us.

"Spiritual Warfare"

This isn't the way most people teach "spiritual warfare." Many folks say, "There's a system of demonic powers hovering over every city. They can block your prayers and prevent them from getting to God. Since the Lord dwells out in space somewhere and the demonic powers are in the physical atmosphere, you have to get your prayers up through them." You may think this sounds silly, but it really is a prevalent doctrine in the body of Christ today. People really believe that you have to clear a hole over your house and/or city so your prayers can get through to God. This is not what the Word of God teaches.

God's Word teaches that the Lord in all of His power and glory indwells each believer. You don't need your prayers to get through the atmosphere, above the ceiling, or even above your nose. The reason you bow your head to pray is so that you can look at God—He lives right there inside you.

These popular, but erroneous, concepts concerning "spiritual warfare" simply don't take into account the New Testament believer being God-possessed. He dwells on the inside of us. Therefore, we don't have to deal with principalities and powers blocking our prayers from getting to God. The way these demons fight us is through our thoughts. The spiritual warfare in the Christian life is in your mind.

There's actually a group here where I live that teaches that when they first arrived in town, the heavens were "brass"—meaning that people's prayers were hindered and they weren't getting through. So through this group's "spiritual warfare" and "intercession," they "opened up the heavens" and cleared things up. They say that's the reason their church has grown and we've seen great things happen in our city. They claim that's why the crime rate dropped for a couple of years in a row. They believe that it's all this intercession and prayer that was making all of this come to pass.

What happened the next year when the crime rate shot back up and there were more murders than ever before? Did the heavens close back up? Did they quit praying effectively? What happened? I recognize that there are many things that influence this, and that Christians do affect the world around them, but it's not all the demons hovering over our city that make a bunch of crime and murders happen.

Battle for the Mind

Why are there lots of homicides in certain places? It's because of the demonic activity in the minds of people, not in the heavenlies. They have lost the battle for their mind and have given themselves over to Satan. They are watching and listening to all kinds of hatred, violence, and murder on television, movies, and video games. Since our society as a whole no longer supports and reinforces godly moral values, we're allowing these things to happen.

Yes, there are demonic powers in the air. Scripture plainly reveals this. But the way we deal with them is by coming against the unrenewed minds of people. Preach and teach the truth of God's Word to people. You can't just control demonic powers in the heavenlies through your prayers, and therefore indirectly control other people and make them not be bad because you are binding a certain demonic power. That's not the model the Scripture presents. The way the Bible teaches us to do it is to go in and tell people the truth. As they believe and obey the truth, they are set free and come out from under the control of these demonic influences that are around us.

There are zero—not just a few, not one, but zero—New Testament precedents for the "spiritual warfare" and intercessory battles that are being promoted in the body of Christ today. Jesus never sent His disciples out to do "spiritual warfare" before He came into a place. He did send them out at times to announce His coming, but this was mainly just publicity.

Paul never called upon or encouraged the believers to do "spiritual warfare" as it's being promoted today. He's the one through whom the Holy Spirit wrote 2 Corinthians 10:3–5 and Ephesians 6:11. Second Corinthians 10 reveals that our weapons are for taking every thought captive to Christ. Ephesians 6:11 tells us to stand against the wiles of the devil. The wrestling mentioned in the very next verse takes place in our thoughts. (Eph. 6:12.)

Influenced Through Thoughts

In our country, morals have decreased significantly in the last generation. The sexual immorality that's being promoted today couldn't have even been imagined thirty years ago. One of the main reasons for this decline is because our culture has become so addicted to radio, television, computers, and movies. Through these mediums, our morals have been steadily polluted and diluted.

Satan has touched individuals who control the media. Both Christians and non-Christians alike are watching the same ungodly media. Therefore, the devil is exercising influence through the thoughts he is planting in us. Satan has to flow through physical things to control the way you think (Rom. 8:6; Prov. 23:7; Isa. 26:3).

Romans 12:2 says, "Be not conformed to this world: but be ye transformed." How? By "spiritual warfare" and binding demons? No, "By the renewing of your mind, that ye may prove what is that good, and acceptable, and perfect, will of God."

Demons influence us through thoughts, but they can't just give those thoughts directly. They have to influence a person, and then that person yields to Satan. He begins to educate them, putting his lies and deception in their life, so they can go out and influence other people. The reason we see such a dominance of ungodly perspectives and principles today is that—as a whole—the news media, television, radio, and the movie industry are controlled by people who are under the influence of Satan. They are demonic in their attitudes and thoughts.

I read an article in which a prominent movie/television producer admitted that one of his goals is to change our country's morals. He is purposefully using his power and influence to change the Judeo-Christian ethic and morality of our culture. Satan is gaining control and exerting influence because he's fighting for people's minds while the church is in their prayer closet trying to bind some demonic power. There is zero scriptural precedent for that. It's not the way they approached this in the Bible.

"Lord, Grant Us Boldness"

The apostle Paul went into terrible demonic places like Corinth and Athens. They had many different pagan gods and idols. He didn't counter all this idolatry by doing "spiritual warfare"—getting a bunch of Christians together and binding something. In Athens, he went into the marketplace and spoke to these people who did nothing but sit around trying to learn something new. Once he had their attention, he preached the Gospel and told them about the unknown God, the One they didn't truly understand. Paul declared, "He's the One, the only true God."

Paul went into Ephesus and shared God's Word. As I mentioned in chapter 14, back then, Ephesus was the location of the famous Diana of the Ephesians. In this temple, there was a statue that they believed fell down from heaven. Paul countered these deceptions and lies by telling people the truth. So many folks responded to the truth that the worship of Diana of the Ephesians literally ceased to be. They closed the temple down and there has never been any demonic power operating through Diana of the Ephesians until the late 1900s when the "intercessors" resurrected her and made her the demonic power operating behind Islam.

A few years ago, over 20,000 people traveled to Ephesus to do "spiritual warfare" and "bind" these demonic powers. Neither Jesus, Peter, nor Paul ever did that. They didn't encourage it. They never gathered people together to bind all the demonic powers in an area. They put their effort into preaching the Gospel and sharing God's Word. They prayed like the early believers in Acts 4.

> Lord, behold their threatenings: and grant unto thy servants, that with all boldness they may speak thy word, by stretching forth thine hand to heal; and that signs and wonders may be done by the name of thy holy child Jesus.
>
> Acts 4:29,30

Then the place was shaken by the power of the Holy Spirit, and they went out boldly sharing the Gospel. (v. 31.) Peter's shadow fell on people as he walked by on the street and they were healed. (Acts 5:15–16.) Signs and wonders confirmed their preaching of the Word. (v. 12; Mark 16:20.) They saw their world changed—not through "spiritual warfare" and "intercession," but through the preaching of the Gospel.

Declaw Satan

There are some Christians today who claim to be called to the "ministry of intercession." This is their whole life. They don't do anything else. They don't share the truth. They don't witness. They don't talk to people. They don't support social action. All they do is stay in their closets and pray.

Now, every believer ought to pray. It's an important part of an intimate relationship with God. I'm not against prayer, but there isn't any such thing as a "ministry of intercession." We're all supposed to pray, but we're all supposed to go out and do something too. Some people are using "intercession" as a cop-out to keep from sharing the Word of God.

The way people are born again is through a seed of God's Word being planted in them. (1 Peter 1:23.) If Satan can deceive us and keep us from sharing God's Word, this is to his advantage. The enemy's strategy is to keep us in a prayer closet, begging the Lord to do what He's told us to do. Instead of boldly sharing the Word and preaching the Gospel, we're afraid to tell anyone the truth because we might offend somebody.

The devil doesn't mind you praying as long as you're into this "spiritual warfare" and "intercession" stuff. Satan himself has inspired much of it. He has you out there fighting a ghost figure. It's as if the devil is projecting a hologram and causing you to see an enemy coming in a certain area. So you marshal all of your forces to fight this enemy that doesn't even exist. You exert a tremendous amount of effort and resources battling this ghost figure and it makes you vulnerable in the areas where dangers do exist. Satan has the body of Christ busy fighting battles and tearing things down that don't even exist. Sure Satan exists and his power exists, but he's not this all-powerful force that the intercessors have made him out to be.

> Your adversary the devil, as a roaring lion, walketh about, seeking whom he may devour.
>
> 1 PETER 5:8

Satan doesn't have the power to control people. He's using nothing but the same human power and authority that were given to mankind. Therefore, he can't do anything to you without your consent and cooperation. Yes, we have an enemy who would like to destroy mankind as a whole, and each of us individually. How do we deal with this? Do we go directly to the devil and bind him? No. We deal with our thoughts. Satan can only influence us and gain our consent and cooperation through our thoughts. That's the reason Jesus said:

> Ye shall know the truth, and the truth shall make you free.
>
> JOHN 8:32

The only power Satan has is in lies and deception. That's the reason the truth makes you free. Once you know the truth, deception no longer has any power. It's declawed. The church's strength is in preaching the Gospel and sharing God's Word.

Demons Were Present

We do need to pray so we can be sensitive to God, yield to Him, hear clearly, and be bold to speak, but we don't need to do fifteen to twenty hours worth of "spiritual warfare" to prepare things before. Just go in and preach the Gospel. The Word of God will change the atmosphere. As you preach the truth, the truth will cause demons to flee. Jesus would walk into a place and the demons would literally cry out, run out, and come out of people. Now, if Jesus had been doing "spiritual warfare" the way it's promoted today, there wouldn't have been any demons to cry out or come out. He would have already dealt with them in prayer and they would have already been gone. But the truth is, demons were present.

Demons were even present at the last supper. How else could Satan have entered into Judas Iscariot if he wasn't already there?

> And after the sop [piece of bread that Jesus gave Judas] Satan entered into him.
>
> John 13:27

That's what the Bible says. Jesus didn't do "spiritual warfare" the way it's being promoted today. It's been given a status and a position that it never should have had. There's a lot of weirdness going on in the body of Christ nowadays in the name of "spiritual warfare."

If Jesus couldn't keep Satan out of His last supper with His disciples, then you can't keep the devil out of your church or city by your "spiritual warfare."

If the Lord were to tarry another hundred years, people would look back on the "spiritual warfare" and "intercession" teachings of our day and think, *Surely that was one of the greatest errors that has ever crept into the body of Christ.* We're so close to it right now and it's so prevalent and popular in the body of Christ, many people don't see it for what it is.

There is no New Testament model for this "spiritual warfare" and "intercession" belief and practice. Some of this is being taught from

Scripture, but they're using Old Testament scriptures—and there's a huge difference between the way things were done in the Old Testament and the way they are done in the New Testament.

CHAPTER 24

One Mediator

Exodus 32 is an Old Testament passage that is often cited when people teach "spiritual warfare" and "intercession." Moses had been up on the mount receiving the Ten Commandments. He'd been up there fasting for forty days and forty nights in the presence of God. After he'd been given these two tablets that had literally been written on by the finger of God:

> The LORD said unto Moses, Go, get thee down; for thy people, which thou broughtest out of the land of Egypt, have corrupted themselves.
>
> EXODUS 32:7

It's interesting how the Lord told Pharaoh through Moses, "Let *My* people go." Yet once the Israelites came out and started worshiping the golden calf they had made (Ex. 32:1–6), He told Moses, "This is *your* people." When a child does something good and wins an award, their parents say, "*My* child." But when the child does something that isn't smart, one parent will say to the other, "Look what *your* child did." God said, "Your people" to Moses. God was ticked off at them because they had corrupted themselves. In fact, He was willing to forsake them and let them go.

> They have turned aside quickly out of the way which I commanded them: they have made them a molten calf, and have worshipped it, and have sacrificed thereunto, and said, These be thy gods, O Israel, which have brought thee up out of the land of Egypt. And the LORD said unto Moses, I have seen this people, and, behold, it is a stiffnecked people: Now therefore let me alone, that my wrath may wax hot against them, and that I may consume them: and I will make of thee a great nation.
>
> EXODUS 32:8–10

Power With God

God was mad at these people. He was going to destroy them and start over with Moses, making a brand-new nation out of him. Notice how God said this:

> Now therefore let me alone, that my wrath may wax hot against them, and that I may consume them.
>
> EXODUS 32:10

The Lord was saying, "Moses, don't try to hinder Me. Don't try to talk Me out of this. Don't plead for mercy because I want to give total vent to My wrath and destroy these people." By saying it this way, God meant, "Moses, you have so much power and influence with Me that if you plead with Me, you'll keep Me from venting my anger on these people."

It's amazing that Almighty God would be moved by any physical human being. It's not that we are greater in power or authority; it's due to His great love for us. Moses wasn't perfect. He had killed a man thinking he was bringing God's will to pass. He had failed. However, God loves us so much that when He finds someone who has a heart for Him, He respects that person. By doing so, that gives the individual power and authority in His life. That's awesome!

> Moses besought the LORD his God, and said, LORD, why doth thy wrath wax hot against thy people, which thou hast brought forth out of the land of Egypt with great power, and with a mighty hand?
>
> EXODUS 32:11

"They're Your People"

Moses put it back on God, saying, "Lord, these are Your people. They aren't my people. Remember, You're the One who redeemed them. They're Your people."

> Wherefore should the Egyptians speak, and say, For mischief did he bring them out, to slay them in the mountains, and to consume them from the face of the earth? Turn from thy fierce wrath, and repent of this evil against thy people. Remember Abraham, Isaac, and Israel, thy servants, to whom thou swarest by thine own self, and saidst unto them, I will multiply your seed as the stars of heaven, and all this land that I have spoken of will I give unto your seed, and they shall inherit it for ever.
>
> EXODUS 32:12,13

Moses was reasoning with God, saying, "LORD, the Egyptians are going to hear about this. They'll say they were destroyed because You were too weak to bring these people into the Promised Land." We saw earlier that Moses had the audacity to say:

> Turn from thy fierce wrath, and repent of this evil against thy people.
>
> EXODUS 32:12

It's amazing that a man would tell God to repent. Yet, what's even more amazing is:

> The LORD repented of the evil which he thought to do unto his people.
>
> EXODUS 32:14

A Classic Example

This is a classic example of Old Testament intercession. Moses confronted God, told Him to turn from His fierce wrath, and He did. Moses stood in between the people who were about to be destroyed and pled with an angry God to repent.

People take this example and use it to teach "spiritual warfare" and "intercession." Thinking this is how we need to pray to God today, they say, "Oh, Lord. Don't destroy our country. Have mercy on our city. Repent, and turn from Your fierce wrath!" That was appropriate for Moses to pray because Christ hadn't come yet and suffered the punishment for our sin. Now under the New Covenant, everything has changed. Jesus became the Intercessor to end all of that kind of intercession.

> There is one God, and one mediator between God and men, the man Christ Jesus.
>
> 1 TIMOTHY 2:5

In the New Testament, Jesus became the Mediator that stood between us and God.

Antichrist

God was holy, and man was not. We deserved the wrath of God. There needed to be mediation between God and man. So before Jesus came, Moses was a mediator. Speaking of Moses, Galatians 3 says that the Old Testament law:

> Was ordained by angels in the hand of a mediator.
>
> GALATIANS 3:19

Moses served as a mediator between God and man. A *mediator* is someone who stands in between two parties who are in conflict with each other and tries to bring them into harmony and agreement. God was opposed to man because of our sin, so under the Old Covenant, Moses served as a mediator. He said, "God, repent. Turn from Your fierce wrath," and God did. However, if Moses were to pray that way today on this side of the cross, he'd be antichrist.

Antichrist means against or instead of Christ. If Moses were to plead with God to turn from His fierce wrath today, he'd be acting against Jesus' mediation. By thinking, *What Christ did is not enough; I need to add to it,* he'd be trying to take Jesus' place. It was appropriate for Moses to pray the way he did under the Old Covenant because Jesus hadn't come yet. But now that Jesus has come and we're under the New Covenant, there's only *one* mediator between God and man—the Lord Jesus Christ. (1 Tim. 2:5.)

That's why you're wrong to "intercede," begging and pleading with God for His mercy today. God's mercy has already been poured out to us through the Lord Jesus Christ. He's no longer angry with us over sin.

For additional study on this topic, I refer you to my teaching entitled, *The War Is Over.* The New Testament is clear. Jesus bore the wrath of God for our sin. That's why God's not mad at you—He isn't even in a bad mood!

A Major Difference

I understand that the truths I'm sharing are contrary to what's been popularly accepted, but I encourage you to go to the Word and see for yourself. Many people think that God is angry at a certain country and that He's about to bring judgment upon a specific city so they pray, "Oh Lord, have mercy and don't destroy them." If you're praying that way, you're trying to take the place of the Lord

Jesus Christ. Jesus has already satisfied God's anger and secured His mercy for these people and places.

Since God's wrath toward sin has been appeased through the sacrifice of Christ, does that mean we don't have any problems? Of course not! Through sin and unbelief, we're in the process of destroying ourselves. We've opened up doors to the devil and he's taking full advantage of them. It's very appropriate to pray, "Father, I thank You that Jesus has already secured Your mercy and grace on our behalf. Thank You that You aren't out to destroy our city and country. However, we're giving place to the devil. We're about to destroy ourselves. So Father, please give me wisdom and boldness to share Your Word and demonstrate Your power to others."

That's the reason I'm on radio, television, and the Internet. That's why I'm putting out so many books, tapes, and CDs. I'm not just praying and asking, "Oh God, do something. Change these places and have mercy on us." God has already had mercy on us. We just don't know what He's done. We've been lied to. Most people are more moved by television, news programs, and movies than they are by the Word of God. They don't know the truth, so I'm using every medium I can to come across people's paths and share the Word with them. These truths are changing people's lives and facilitating revival. Revival comes through people as the Gospel is preached, the Word is taught, and the Holy Spirit confirms it.

There is a major difference between the Old and New Covenants. In the Old Testament, people like Moses pled with God, saying, "Lord, turn from Your fierce wrath." But in the New Testament, there's only one mediator between God and man, Christ Jesus. He has forever satisfied the demands and wrath of God. If we don't seek God, there will be plenty of problems. But that's because we're yielding ourselves to Satan, and he's going to steal, kill, and destroy whomever, whenever, and wherever he can. (John 10:10.) Yes, our city needs to change. Yes, our country needs to repent and turn to God. But it's not so we won't be judged. Since God has already placed upon His Son the judgment our sins deserved, we don't have to be judged.

Apologize to Whom?

I didn't understand these truths when I first started out in ministry. I liked to say, "If God doesn't judge our country, He's going to have to apologize to Sodom and Gomorrah." From my perspective, America deserved judgment because of our sin as much or more than these two Old Testament cities that went up in smoke. Since then, however, God has revealed Himself and His Word to me in such a way that I now say, "If God were to judge our country, He'd have to apologize to Jesus." Why? The reason is that Christ bore our punishment, judgment, and separation so that we wouldn't have to. God has already placed His wrath upon His own Son at the cross, so He's not about to judge us.

Our country is perilously close to being destroyed—not because of God's judgment, but because of Satan's inroads. When you yield yourself to the devil through sin, you become his defenseless servant. Remember, he comes for no other purpose but to steal, kill, and destroy. It's stupid to yield to Satan. We need to submit ourselves to God.

"Will You Spare the City?"

Let's take a closer look at when God judged the cities of Sodom and Gomorrah. First, the Lord appeared to Abraham and told him He was sending two angels down to Sodom and Gomorrah to check the cities out. God wanted to see if they were as bad as He had heard because He planned to judge them. As soon as Abraham heard about this, he:

> Drew near, and said, Wilt thou also destroy the righteous with the wicked? Peradventure there be fifty righteous within the city: wilt thou also destroy and not spare the place for the fifty righteous that are therein? That be far from thee to do after this manner, to slay the righteous with the wicked: and that the righteous should be as the wicked, that be far from thee: Shall not the Judge of all the earth do right? And the LORD said, If I find in Sodom fifty righteous within the city, then I will spare all the place for their sakes.
>
> GENESIS 18:23–26

Here's Abraham pleading with God and saying, "LORD, You aren't going to destroy the righteous people that live in this city too, are You? That's not the way a righteous God would act. If there's fifty righteous people there, will You spare the city?"

And God answered, "If there's fifty righteous people, I'll spare the city."

Then Abraham said, "What if there's forty-five righteous people? Will You spare the city?"

"If there's forty-five, I'll spare the city."

Abraham negotiated with God all the way down to ten. If there were ten righteous people, God would spare the city. Abraham could have gone all the way down to one righteous person, and that would have been Lot. (2 Peter 2:7–8.)

Without even factoring Jesus' atonement into the equation and forgetting about the New Covenant—which most Christians tend to do anyway—this passage shows us that God won't destroy a city or country if there are righteous people therein. It doesn't matter what your country is, there are things in it that are completely contrary to the kingdom of God. Nobody's country is living totally the way God wants us to. Yet, despite all this, there are righteous people now in every country of the world. That alone ought to debunk much of this "God's going to judge this country" teaching that's floating around the body of Christ today. In America alone, there are hundreds of thousands of righteous, born-again people who love God and are seeking Him. We may not be dominating in every area of society yet, but we're here. So God will not destroy us.

New Testament Reality

We also need to factor into this equation the truth of 1 Timothy 2:5. Jesus is now the one and only mediator between God and man. He forever satisfied God's wrath. In light of these truths, this whole pattern of Old Covenant intercession—begging God not to pour out His wrath and pleading with Him for mercy—doesn't fit the New Testament reality.

Most of the "spiritual warfare" and "intercession" ideas that people are promoting come from the Old Covenant. They're taking Old Testament scriptures and teaching them just as if Jesus Christ had never come. Basically, they're saying, "You be a mediator. You stand between God and man. You plead with Him to turn from His wrath. Don't allow Him to judge this land." Well, the truth is that Jesus Christ has already done all those things. He is the *only* New Testament mediator.

If you're trying to pray the same as Abraham in Genesis 18, you're standing against what Jesus has already done. If you're praying the same as Moses in Exodus 32, then you're trying to take Christ's place. You are acting as if Jesus hasn't come and His atonement wasn't enough. You're believing that His intercession wasn't enough, and you have to add to it. That's antichrist.

CHAPTER 25

The Battle is in Your Mind

Concerning the believer's authority, we need to recognize that Satan has already been dealt with by God. Since Jesus endured God's wrath at the cross, He isn't pouring it out upon us today. Our job is to stand in faith and enforce what the Lord has already done through His death, burial, and resurrection. One way we do this is by telling people the truth.

The battle is in your mind. Satan isn't controlling people through some demonic power. He's controlling them through lies and deceptions. By telling the truth, lies are exposed and people are set free. So much of this "spiritual warfare" and "intercession" teaching denies the ministry of the Lord Jesus Christ. That's not smart.

Jesus is the New Testament Intercessor who ended all Old Covenant intercession. There's now no need to beg for mercy or to tell God to repent. New Testament believers praise God for what He's already done and offer themselves as a vessel for the Lord to work through.

The real focus needs to be on the way we think. Don't just pray for someone and wait on God to touch that person without human intervention. God flows through people. He uses us. We must preach the Gospel.

> How then shall they call on him in whom they have not believed? and how shall they believe in him of whom they have not heard? and how shall they hear without a preacher? And how shall they preach, except they be sent?...So then faith cometh by hearing, and hearing by the word of God.
>
> ROMANS 10:14,15,17

You can't just pray and get a person saved, healed, or anything. You must speak God's Word. Faith for salvation, healing, and everything else comes by hearing the Word of God.

"Stop the Plague!"

Numbers 16 is another Old Testament example that is often used to teach "spiritual warfare" and "intercession." People say, "You must stand in the gap, begging and pleading with God for your loved ones to be saved, healed, or whatever." This passage of scripture details what happens right after Korah, Dathan, and Abiram rebelled against Moses. The earth opened up and swallowed all three of these men and all that they possessed. (Num. 16:32–33.) Of course, the people just screamed and ran for fear.

> But on the morrow all the congregation of the children of Israel murmured against Moses and against Aaron, saying, Ye have killed the people of the LORD. And it came to pass, when the congregation was gathered against Moses and against Aaron, that they looked toward the tabernacle of the congregation: and, behold, the cloud covered it, and the glory of the LORD appeared. And Moses and Aaron came before the tabernacle of the congregation. And the LORD spake unto Moses, saying, Get you up from among this congregation, that I may consume them as in a moment. And they fell upon their faces.
>
> NUMBERS 16:41–45

God was upset because the people had come against Moses and Aaron.

> Moses said unto Aaron, Take a censer, and put fire therein from off the altar, and put on incense, and go quickly unto the congregation, and make an atonement for them: for there is wrath gone out from the LORD; the plague is begun. And Aaron took as Moses commanded, and ran into the midst of the congregation; and, behold, the plague was begun among the people: and he put on incense, and made an atonement for the people. And he stood between the dead and the living; and the plague was stayed. Now they that died in the plague were fourteen thousand and seven hundred, beside them that died about the matter of Korah.
>
> NUMBERS 16:46–49

This is another example of where God became angry with the children of Israel. Moses recognized it, and told Aaron to take a censer and put coals from off of the altar on it (symbolic of prayer). He took this censer—prayer—and stood—interceded—between those who had already died of the plague and those who hadn't. Once the plague reached where he stood offering prayers and intercession, it stopped. However, 14,700 people died before Aaron could run in there with this censer and stop the plague.

I've literally heard people teaching on "intercession" say, "This is the way it is. God is holy and man isn't. He's so angry at people that He's about to destroy them. God is sending hurricanes, tornadoes, tsunamis, AIDS, and all kinds of tragedies. God's wrath has begun, and we as intercessors need to pray and stand between God and these people who are deserving of His wrath. We need to plead for mercy, calm Him down, and beg Him to sit back down on the throne so He won't destroy the human race." People are preaching such nonsense.

A Much Better Job

Jesus is the only mediator now between God and man. (1 Tim. 2:5.) There's no other mediator and no other mediation that needs to be done. When Jesus died, He forever satisfied the wrath of God. The Lord isn't ready to destroy this nation or any other. I'm not saying we don't deserve it. I'm saying God placed the punishment for our rebellion and sins upon Jesus. He's not giving us what we deserve. It's not God who is about to destroy this nation or city.

As an individual, you may feel like you deserve the wrath of God. You don't doubt that God exists. You just don't think He'll do anything for you because you know you aren't living life the way you should. God is speaking to you right now, saying, "Jesus has already borne your punishment. He's already suffered your pain. I'm not the one bringing tragedy into your life." You might be thinking, *But I have all kinds of problems. Surely, God is judging me.* No, you yielded yourself to Satan and he comes to steal, kill, and destroy. (John 10:10.) So yes, your life may be a mess—but it's not because God's wrath is upon you and He's judging you.

God placed His wrath over your sins upon Jesus, and all you must do is humble yourself and receive the forgiveness He offers as a free gift. You don't have to beg and plead with the Lord to save you. He's already done it. He's already dealt with your sin through the atoning sacrifice of His Son.

You don't need to beg and plead on an individual basis or on a collective basis (for a city or country). God's wrath has been satisfied. If you're trying to tell God to repent and have mercy, then you're trying to improve upon the work that the Lord Jesus Christ has already done. I guarantee that Jesus did a much better job at it than what you could ever do.

Powerful Proof

You don't need to plead with God to turn His heart toward us. His heart is already toward us because He loves us. This country is in the process of being destroyed because of our own wickedness and yielding to Satan. However, God wants to redeem this country and see us wholeheartedly turn back to Him. He needs Christians to come out of their prayer closets and stop begging Him for what Jesus has already provided. He needs believers to stand up in faith and start taking this good news to others: "God isn't mad. He's not even in a bad mood. God isn't ticked off. He loves you and wants you to be free." Tell people the truth because it's the truth that will set them free. (John 8:32.)

It's not up to God whether the lost get saved or not. He's already made the atonement and paid for their sins. He's extended forgiveness and abundant life, but they aren't receiving. He's sent the Holy Spirit to deal with people and convict them, but they're resisting Him. One of the biggest reasons people aren't making the right choice is because they aren't hearing the good news of the Gospel. They're being lied to by the devil.

Although Satan is inspiring it, people are the ones who are saying, "There are no absolutes. Sexual immorality isn't wrong. There are many roads to heaven," and such. Through these lies, people have dropped their guard and stopped resisting evil. They've embraced sin, and because of it have welcomed Satan right into their life. He's blinded their hearts from the light of Christ (2 Cor. 4:4), but the antidote isn't doing "spiritual warfare," binding demons, and begging God. It's us standing up, preaching the Gospel, and telling people the truth.

God always backs up His truth with power. (Mark 16:20.) We need to believe the Word and trust the Holy Spirit to demonstrate that power. Jesus had to have miracles to validate what He was saying. He told the religious Jews that if they couldn't believe because of His words, then to believe because of His miracles. (John 10:38.) If Jesus needed to have proof for people to believe that He was sent from God and speaking the truth, then we do too. We need to start sharing God's Word and demonstrating His supernatural power. Then people will turn to the Lord.

Share the Truth

One time I met a woman before a meeting in Birmingham who had just been in the hospital. She'd been laying flat on her back watching me say these things on television. The doctors had given her up to die. Just a year before, her mother had passed away from the same exact thing—cancer. This woman wasn't only sick in her body, but also sick in her heart and mind. She was hopeless and fearful because she'd seen other people die of the same disease and the doctors had told her there was nothing they could do. As she lay there on the hospital bed, she saw that I was going to be in Birmingham, so she pulled the tubes out of her body, checked herself out of the hospital, and came to my meeting to receive prayer.

I prayed with her and she was instantly healed. Every bit of pain and all the cancer's symptoms were gone. At the end of the service, I gave an invitation for people to be born again. Since she'd never received the Lord, she came forward, gave her life to Jesus, and was born again. She got healed, delivered of cancer, born again, baptized in the Holy Spirit, and spoke in tongues all in one night. She checked into a nearby hotel and stayed for the next three days' worth of meetings, getting built up in her faith. All this came to pass because she heard the truth and saw the power of God in demonstration.

Some of the doctrines that are held most dear in the body of Christ today have been established by the devil. (1 Tim. 4:1.) These lies have been rendering us ineffective. This woman in Birmingham didn't get healed through somebody interceding for her in some closet. She heard a believer speaking the truth and giving testimonies of what God had done. The Holy Spirit used these things to quicken her faith. A woman—who wasn't even born again yet—pulled the tubes out of her body, walked out of the hospital, and came to where the believers were meeting.

Faith came to her by hearing, and hearing by the Word of God. (Rom. 10:17.) When the truth comes to people, it begins to tear down the lies, deceptions, and strongholds of the devil. Faith can't rise in someone's heart unless you share the truth with them.

God told Jeremiah:

> Behold, I will make my words in thy mouth fire, and this people wood, and it shall devour them…Is not my word like as a fire? saith the LORD; and like a hammer that breaketh the rock in pieces?
>
> JEREMIAH 5:14; 23:29

This is the reason we must speak the Word. Somehow or another, we've gotten away from this. We've been diverted and distracted, putting so much of our energy into begging God to do what He's already done. That's ineffective. We've been in prayer closets binding Satan and commanding him to let people go, thinking that if we pray hard enough people will get born again. That's not true. The Word says that people must be born again by the incorruptible seed of God's Word. (1 Pet. 1:23.)

CHAPTER 26

Fight to Win!

I've received many benefits through understanding the believer's authority. I've realized that Satan doesn't have the power to make me do anything. This old saying, "The devil made me do it" is absolutely wrong. Satan can't make you do anything. All he can do is lie to you. Then, if you believe his lie, you empower him to accomplish his will. But he can't do anything to you without your consent and cooperation. This is the reason the battle isn't against demonic powers directly. Satan has been stripped. His only power is deception.

That's how he came against Adam and Eve. Satan didn't come in some intimidating animal like a tiger, bear, or mammoth. He chose the most subtle, cunning, crafty animal and came against them with words—deception. Satan chose the snake because he knew he had no power to force Eve into doing anything. He used words to deceive her.

If Eve would have evaluated those words and refused to allow those ungodly thoughts to influence her, she wouldn't have been tempted. If she would have refused to listen to or think anything that countered what God had said, she wouldn't have committed that sin and plunged the whole human race under the authority and dominion of the devil. This all happened through words, and it's still happening today. Satan is fighting us with words and thoughts.

Choose Wisely

The battle is right between your ears. It's not out there somewhere in the heavenly places. It's in your head. Every word you hear either releases life or death. Words that are based on and are in line with the Word of God release life. Words that are inconsistent with what God says minister death.

> Death and life are in the power of the tongue.
>
> PROVERBS 18:21

It's either life or death, one or the other. What are you listening to? What are you saying?

> But I say unto you, That every idle word that men shall speak, they shall give account thereof in the day of judgment. For by thy words thou shalt be justified, and by thy words thou shalt be condemned.
>
> MATTHEW 12:36,37

Every word you speak and every word you hear are either producing life or death. Everything you listen to on radio, television, or movies is ministering either life or death. If you disagree with these truths from God's Word, you're deceived.

> Be not deceived: evil communications corrupt good manners.
>
> 1 CORINTHIANS 15:33

I'm not suggesting that you move into a monastery and take a vow of silence. I'm encouraging you to recognize life and death, and to exercise more self-control in what you're choosing. Every television and radio I've ever seen had an On/Off knob and multiple stations to choose from. You don't have to sit in front of the set and just passively take whatever is offered to you. Choose wisely.

I have to deal with this the same as anybody else. There have been times when I've had nothing specific to do. I've wanted to kick back and relax a bit, so I've turned on the television. I've flipped through the channels and nothing was on—what's new?—but I ended up watching something just for the sake of watching it, not realizing that it was pouring junk in me.

You need to recognize that Satan is fighting you with negative words. You can't change the fact that every word you hear is either releasing death or life, but you can change whether you listen to it or not. You don't have to swallow it and believe it. You can get to where you're constantly listening to words that minister life, but the choice is up to you.

Renew Your Mind

> Grace and peace be multiplied unto you through the knowledge of God, and of Jesus our Lord.
>
> 2 Peter 1:2

It's through the knowledge of God that grace and peace are multiplied unto us. Satan knows this, which is why he battles us in our mind.

> Be not conformed to this world: but be ye transformed by the renewing of your mind.
>
> Romans 12:2

Metamorphoo is the Greek word rendered "transformed."[1] It's where we get the English word "metamorphosis." If you want to change from being something creepy, crawly, and earthbound into something beautiful that can fly, then you need to renew your mind.

Many people are trying to take a shortcut. They keep their mind in the gutter, listening to all the things of the world. They allow the sewage of this world to flow through them, but they want the results that God produces. They think, *If I just pray and ask, I can receive.* There's more to it than just praying and believing. You must also cooperate with God's spiritual laws. God operates through us when we get our heart and mind stayed upon Him. However, Satan hinders God through our thoughts.

Word-Minded

> To be carnally minded is death; but to be spiritually minded is life and peace.
>
> ROMANS 8:6

If you want to experience life and peace, then you need to become spiritually minded. Jesus said:

> The words that I speak unto you, they are spirit, and they are life.
>
> JOHN 6:63

Being spiritually minded is being Word-minded. It's thinking on what God has to say about your situation instead of what the world has to say. If you are Word-minded, you'll have life and peace. Grace and peace will be multiplied to you as you continually think on the knowledge of God. You can't think negatively—adopting the mindset of the world—and then experience the life, grace, and peace of God. It doesn't work that way.

I get nearly all of my news off the little three-minute news bites on the radio. I hardly watch any television. I figure if something is really that important, it'll make the radio news bites. I've come to the place where I can pretty much handle three minutes of anything negative that the world has to say. But even in those three little minutes, so much of what they say is based on fear, doubt, and unbelief. If you swallow all of that, you'll be in turmoil. But if you listen to and go by the Word of God, you'll have life, grace, and peace.

Through God's Word, I know I'm protected.

> No weapon that is formed against thee shall prosper; and every tongue that shall rise against thee in judgment thou shalt condemn. This is the heritage of the servants of the LORD, and their righteousness is of me, saith the LORD.
>
> ISAIAH 54:17

Notice that you aren't automatically protected. This verse says that you have to condemn the words that come against you. If you just passively sit there and let these ungodly things be spoken, then they will impact you. (1 Cor. 15:33.) But when you hear something contrary to God's Word, if you will condemn it—recognize it as being wrong and counter it with the truth of the Word—then it becomes powerless.

My wife will tell you that there are many times when I talk back to the television and radio. We'll be listening to the news, and they'll say, "It's flu season." I'll declare, "There is no season where the Word of God doesn't work. By His stripes, I have been healed. I'm not getting the flu!" This is what it means to condemn the words that come against us. Even if many people around me are affected, I'll be safe and sound.

> A thousand shall fall at thy side, and ten thousand at thy right hand; but it shall not come nigh thee. Only with thine eyes shalt thou behold and see the reward of the wicked.
>
> PSALM 91:7,8

In addition to protection, God's Word promises prosperity, healing, and deliverance. If you will keep your mind fixed on God, these promises will work for you. Remind yourself of how God protected, prospered, healed, and delivered other people in the Word. Keep those thoughts in the forefront of your thinking, and you'll have peace. But if you allow your mind to go the way the world is thinking—fear, doubt, and unbelief—you'll have all those things instead. It really is this simple.

The Antidote to Any Problem

Grace and peace come through the way you think. Think properly, and you'll have grace, joy, life, and peace. These don't come by prayer, but through the knowledge of God.

> According as his divine power hath given unto us *all things* that pertain unto life and godliness, through the knowledge of him that hath called us to glory and virtue.
>
> 2 PETER 1:3

All things that pertain to life and godliness come through the knowledge of God. It's not "some things" or "a few things," but *"all things."* This means that if you are sick in your body, you have a knowledge problem. If you're poor, you have a knowledge problem. If you're depressed, you have a knowledge problem. The antidote to any problem is the knowledge of God.

Most people don't believe that. They think that if you have an emotional problem, you go take a pill for it. "This problem has nothing to do with me and my choices. I don't have any responsibility whatsoever. It's just the way my hormones are—my chemistry. It's what so-and-so did to me." All of these excuses are wrong in light of God's Word. You need to accept responsibility, go to the Bible, and start thinking according to the Word. (Isa. 26:3.) The key is how you think.

> Whereby are given unto us exceeding great and precious promises: that by these ye might be partakers of the divine nature, having escaped the corruption that is in the world through lust.
>
> 2 PETER 1:4

Through the knowledge of God, we are given exceedingly great and precious promises. The Word of God is the knowledge of God. It's God's thoughts. These promises are the knowledge of God. We become partakers of God's divine nature and escape the corruption that is in the world through lust by the knowledge of God—not through begging for it in prayer or pleading for God to move. You must get your thinking straightened out. (Prov. 23:7.)

What Is Your Mind Full Of?

You can't be tempted with something you don't think.

> Truly, if they had been mindful of that country from whence they came out, they might have had opportunity to have returned.
>
> HEBREWS 11:15

This scripture is talking about Abraham and Sarah. They used to live in Ur of the Chaldees, which was in the area of Babylon. God told them to leave there and come over into the land we now call Israel. (Gen. 12:1.) He told them that someday they would inherit that land. Abraham actually entered into the Promised Land when he was about seventy-five years old. He lived to be 175 (Gen. 25:7), and never did inherit that promise in his lifetime. He bought a parcel of that land just to be able to bury his wife (Gen. 23:15–19), but it was generations later when the Israelites actually came in and possessed the land.

How did Abraham remain faithful to God's promise—His word to him—for all those years? Hebrews 11:15 says that if they had been mindful—thinking—of the country they came out of they might have had opportunity to have returned. For them, an opportunity to go back to Ur of the Chaldees would have been a temptation to sin. It would have been rebellion against God for them to have returned to their homeland. Their opportunity to sin—temptation—was linked to what they thought.

If you think on things that provide you with temptation, then an opportunity to sin will come. But if you refuse to think on things that gender temptation, you won't be tempted. That's good news! Another way of saying this is: You can't be tempted with what you don't think.

Our culture has convinced us that we need to be "informed" about all of the junk, rottenness, and perversion going on out in the world. God's Word teaches us otherwise.

> I would have you wise unto that which is good, and *simple* concerning evil.
>
> Romans 16:19

We are to be simple—ignorant—of evil. The Lord doesn't want us to be well versed in these things. The original temptation Adam and Eve fell for was the desire to know more—to know good and evil. God had already given them all the knowledge they needed. Everything He told them was good. God doesn't want us to know evil.

Yet, today we feel like we need to know all kinds of evil—what everyone else is doing. By doing so, you open yourself up to temptation. You can't be tempted by what you don't think. We need to win the battle for our mind. We need to quit exposing ourselves to all of the junk that Satan is offering through this world, and get to where all we do is think on God's Word. If the Word of God is all we meditate on, then God's Word is all we'll be tempted with. That's the way it works.

Naïve in New York

I'm a living example of this truth in action. I was raised in a Christian home and just believed what I was told. I don't remember hearing much about adultery, fornication, or sexual immorality except that they were wrong, so I never really thought about it.

When I was eighteen years old, my mother took me to a Billy Graham youth event in Bern, Switzerland. Since we were traveling as part of a group, I stayed with a bunch of guys while Mom was with the other women. Our first stop was New York City. I was plucked out of my controlled environment and planted downtown in a very ungodly city. I was exposed to things I had never seen or heard of before. I didn't even know they existed. Because I was naïve, I wasn't tempted.

I remember walking around 42nd and Broadway, where there was a tremendous amount of prostitution. There must have been about a hundred women lined up along a wall there that night. I didn't have a clue. It never even dawned on me. I never even wondered why they were there. I just thought, *What a great opportunity to witness!* So I took some tracts out and went down the row passing them out and witnessing to each of these prostitutes. I didn't know what they were or why they were standing there, so I wasn't tempted. There I was out on the streets of downtown New York City at two in the morning witnessing to people. I'd never seen that many folks in my life. As a little country boy from Texas, I was pretty shocked.

While out there, a pimp tried to sell me one of his girls. He came up to me and started speaking in street language. I didn't know what he was talking about. Nobody I knew talked that way. This guy tried to sell me for ten minutes, but I didn't understand what he was trying to communicate. Finally, he just looked at me, turned around, threw up his hands, and walked off shaking his head. He was probably wondering, *What rock did this hick crawl out from under?*

Back at the hotel, I told my roommates some of the things this guy had said. They had to explain to me that he was a pimp trying to sell me a prostitute. I was so naïve, I didn't even know what he was talking about. I hadn't thought that way before. I wasn't aware of the terminology. Therefore, I wasn't tempted.

You Can Win

Are you someone who has to fight temptation tooth and nail? Are you holding on with white knuckles, yet you can't understand why it's so hard to live for God? If so, most likely the reason is that you allow so much junk to be planted in you. You're trying to rebuke lust, sexual addiction, and pornography by doing "spiritual warfare" against these demons, yet you're sitting there listening to and watching this garbage every day on television, which encourages sin.

Much of today's television programs will expose you to more sex-related subject matter in an hour's time than your great-grandparents saw their entire lifetime. Even if you find a decent show, usually the commercials will kill you. The average magazine and newspaper isn't much better. They show all degrees of nudity and sexual content. The media bombards us with it on all sides.

The sad thing is that most Christians allow this stuff into their home. They expose their children to it (through television and other medium), and then wonder why they're having problems. They're doing "spiritual warfare" and "intercession" so that their kids will grow up to be godly people, but then they just allow Satan to deposit his perversion and unbelief in them. The devil loves it when parents use the television as a babysitter so they don't have to pay any attention to their kids.

We've allowed things into our lives and then wondered, *Why am I so tempted? Why is the Christian life so hard to live?* It's hard because Satan comes at us through the way we think. He can do nothing to you without your consent and cooperation. We need to start being selective about what we let into our eyes, ears, and hearts.

Your life will go in the direction of your dominant thoughts. Don't let the junk of this world fill your mind. Set your heart to seek the Lord and meditate on His Word. The battle truly is in your mind. You can win this fight, but you must fight to win!

Conclusion

Now that you realize the spiritual dynamics behind what's happening in the physical realm, you recognize that we're truly in a spiritual battle! You understand the spiritual significance of your choices, words, and actions. And you recognize that the battlefield is in your mind. Whom you yield to—God or Satan—is whom you empower to work in and through your life. (Rom. 6:16.) Therefore, submit to God, resist the devil—and he will flee from you! (James 4:7.)

I pray this newfound awareness will motivate you to meditate daily on the truths of God's Word. Let them penetrate your heart and renew your mind. Then you'll find yourself thinking God's thoughts, speaking His Word, and acting in faith. You'll discover more of God's laws and how to cooperate with them. And as you take responsibility to exercise your God-given authority, you'll enjoy more and more of the abundant life Jesus died and resurrected to provide.

Receive Jesus as Your Savior

Choosing to receive Jesus Christ as your Lord and Savior is the most important decision you'll ever make!

God's Word promises, "If thou shalt confess with thy mouth the Lord Jesus, and shalt believe in thine heart that God hath raised him from the dead, thou shalt be saved. For with the heart man believeth unto righteousness; and with the mouth confession is made unto salvation.... For whosoever shall call upon the name of the Lord shall be saved" (Rom. 10:9–10,13).

By His grace, God has already done everything to provide salvation. Your part is simply to believe and receive.

Pray out loud, *Jesus, I confess that You are my Lord and Savior. I believe in my heart that God raised You from the dead. By faith in Your Word, I receive salvation now. Thank You for saving me!*

The very moment you commit your life to Jesus Christ, the truth of His Word instantly comes to pass in your spirit. Now that you're born again, there's a brand-new you!

Receive the Holy Spirit

As His child, your loving heavenly Father wants to give you the supernatural power you need to live this new life.

> For every one that asketh receiveth; and he that seeketh findeth; and to him that knocketh it shall be opened... If ye...know how to give good gifts unto your children: how much more shall your heavenly Father give the Holy Spirit to them that ask him?
>
> LUKE 11:10,13

All you have to do is ask, believe, and receive! Pray, *Father, I recognize my need for Your power to live this new life. Please fill me with Your Holy Spirit. By faith, I receive it right now! Thank You for baptizing me. Holy Spirit, You are welcome in my life.*

Congratulations! Now you're filled with God's supernatural power. Some syllables from a language you don't recognize will rise up from your heart to your mouth. (See 1 Cor. 14:14.) As you speak them out loud by faith, you're releasing God's power from within and building yourself up in the Spirit. (See v. 4.) You can do this whenever and wherever you like.

It doesn't really matter whether you felt anything or not when you prayed to receive the Lord and His Spirit. If you believed in your heart that you received, then God's Word promises you did. "Therefore I say unto you, What things soever ye desire, when ye pray, believe that ye receive them, and ye shall have them" (Mark 11:24). God always honors His Word; believe it!

Please contact me and let me know that you've prayed to receive Jesus as your Savior or to be filled with the Holy Spirit. I would like to rejoice with you and help you understand more fully what has taken place in your life. I'll send you a free gift that will help you understand and grow in your new relationship with the Lord. Welcome to your new life!

Endnotes

Chapter 1

[1] Based on information from Scofield, C.I., *Scofield Reference Notes,* (1917 Edition), "Scofield Reference Notes on Matthew 4," available from http://bible.crosswalk.com/Commentaries/ScofieldReferenceNotes/srn.cgi?book=mt&chapter=004, "possessed with devils," Matthew 4:24.

[2] Based on a information in Thayer and Smith, *The KJV New Testament Greek Lexicon,* "Greek Lexicon entry for Daimonizomai," available from http://www.biblestudytools.net/Lexicons/Greek/grk.cgi?number=1139&version=kjv, s.v. "possessed with devils," Matthew 8:28.

Chapter 2

[1] Thayer and Smith, "Greek Lexicon entry for Katapino," available from http://www.biblestudytools.net/Lexicons/Greek/grk.cgi?number=2666&version=kjv, s.v. "devour," 1 Peter 5:8.

Chapter 4

[1] Well-known preacher and evangelist considered by many to be the father of the "Word of Faith" movement.

Chapter 7

[1] Based on information from Thayer and Smith, "Greek Lexicon entry for Methodeia," available from http://www.biblestudytools.net/Lexicons/Greek/grk.cgi?number=3180&version=kjv, s.v. "wiles," Ephesians 6:11.

[2] "The rudiments of the human nature of Christ was a real creation in the womb of the virgin, by the energy of the Spirit of God." Adam Clarke, *The Adam Clarke Commentary,* "Commentary on Luke 1," available from http://www.studylight.org/com/acc/view.cgi?book=lu&chapter=001, s.v. "Verse 35. The Holy Ghost shall come upon thee," Luke 1:35.

Chapter 12

[1] Based on information from Brown, Driver, Briggs and Gesenius, *The KJV Old Testament Hebrew Lexicon,* "Hebrew Lexicon entry for 'Iy-kabowd," available from http://www.biblestudytools.net/Lexicons/Hebrew/heb.cgi?number=350&version=kjv, s.v. "Ichabod," 1 Samuel 4:21.

Chapter 14

[1] Adam Clarke, available from http://www.studylight.org/com/acc/view.cgi?book=ga&chapter=003, s.v. "It was ordained by angels," Galatians 3:19.

Chapter 15

[1] Azusa Street is where the Pentecostal revival meeting began in the early 1900s, that is credited with being the catalyst for the spread of the Pentecostal movement in the twentieth century.

Chapter 17

[1] Based on information from American Dictionary of the English Language, 10th Ed. (San Francisco: Foundation for American Christian Education, 1998). Fascimile of Noah Webster's 1828 edition, permission to reprint by G.&C. Merriam Company, copyright, 1967 & 1995 (Renewal) by Rosalie J. Slater, s.v. "resist."

Chapter 26

[1] Thayer and Smith, "Greek Lexicon entry for Metamorphoo," available from http://www.biblestudytools.net/Lexicons/Greek/grk.cgi?number=3339&version=kjv, s.v. "transform," Romans 12:2.

About the Author

Andrew's life was forever changed the moment he encountered the supernatural love of God on March 23, 1968. The author of more than thirty books, Andrew has made it his mission for more than five decades to change the way the world sees God.

Andrew's vision is to go as far and deep with the Gospel as possible. His message goes *far* through the *Gospel Truth* television and radio program, which is available to nearly half the world's population. The message goes *deep* through discipleship at Charis Bible College, founded in 1994, which currently has more than seventy campuses and over 6,000 students around the globe. These students will carry on the same mission of changing the way the world sees God. This is Andrew's legacy.

To contact Andrew Wommack please write, e-mail, or call:

Andrew Wommack Ministries, Inc.
P.O. Box 3333 • Colorado Springs, CO 80934-3333
E-mail: info@awmi.net
Helpline Phone (orders and prayer): 719-635-1111
Hours: 4:00 AM to 9:30 PM MST

Andrew Wommack Ministries of Europe
P.O. Box 4392 • WS1 9AR Walsall • England
E-mail: enquiries@awme.net
U.K. Helpline Phone (orders and prayer):
011-44-192-247-3300
Hours: 5:30 AM to 4:00 PM GMT

Or visit him on the Web at: **www.awmi.net**

The War Is Over

Peace has been won. The longest conflict in history lasted 4,000 years and ended in a decisive victory nearly 2,000 years ago. Still, many have not yet heard the news and they continue to fight the battle—the battle of sin and judgment.

On the cross Jesus said "It is finished," victory was declared, and reconciliation began. It was the victory promised when Jesus was born and the angels declared, "Glory to God in the highest, and on earth peace, good will toward men" (Luke 2:14). Is this saying Jesus came to create peace among men? If it is, then He has most certainly failed.

The peace He spoke of was not among men, but between God and man. Sin is no longer the issue; the price has been paid once and for all. God sent His only Son to bear our sin, becoming sin itself, and then judged Him without mercy for that sin. Was His sacrifice enough for you? Is God withholding His blessing because of your sin? If you die with an unconfessed sin, would you be lost? The answers in this book will release you from the condemnation of judgment and fear. It will free you to receive the promised blessings of God!

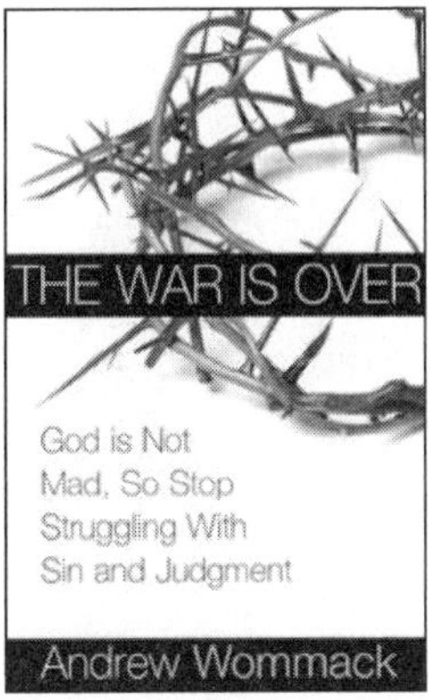

Item Code: 1053-C 5-CD album

Item Code: 1053-D 6-DVD album

ISBN: 1-57794-935-0 Paperback

Available at bookstores everywhere
or visit **www.harrisonhouse.com**

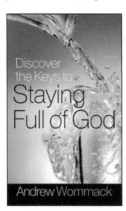

Grace, the Power of the Gospel

Recent surveys indicate that the vast majority of Christians, those claiming to be born again, believe that their salvation is at least in part dependent upon their behavior and actions. Yes, they believe Jesus died for their sin, but once they accept Him as their Savior they believe they must still meet a certain standard to be "good enough." If that is true, then what is that standard and how do you know when you have met it? The Church has tried to answer these questions for centuries always resulting in religious and legalistic bondage.

So what is the answer? First, begin by asking the right question. It is not, "What must we do?" but rather, "What did Jesus do?" By understanding the apostle Paul's revelation in the book of Romans of what Jesus did, you will never again wonder if you're meeting the standard.

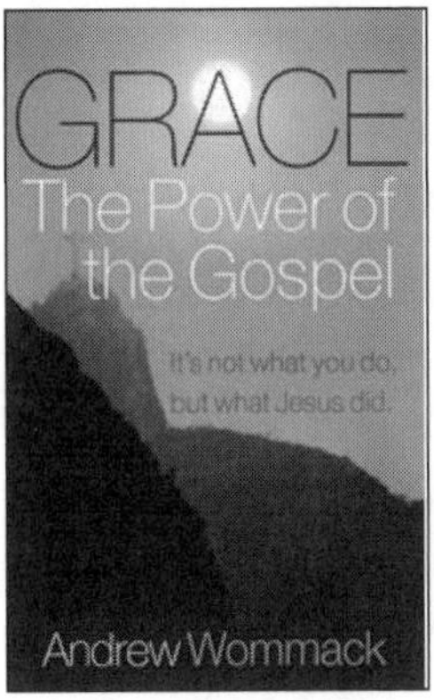

Item Code: 1014-C 4-CD album

Item Code: 1014-D 5-DVD album

ISBN: 1-57794-921-8 Paperback

Other Teachings by Andrew Wommack

Spirit, Soul & Body

Understanding the relationship of your spirit, soul, and body is foundational to your Christian life. You will never truly know how much God loves you or believe what His Word says about you until you do. In this series, learn how spirit, soul and body are related and how that knowledge will release the life of your spirit into your body and soul. It may even explain why many things are not working the way you had hoped.

Item Code: 318 Paperback

Item Code: 1027-C 4-CD album

The True Nature of God

Are you confused about the nature of God? Is He the God of judgment found in the Old Testament or the God of mercy and grace found in the New Testament? Andrew's revelation on this subject will set you free and give you a confidence in your relationship with God like never before. This is truly nearly-too-good-to-be-true news.

Item Code: 308 Paperback

Item Code: 1002-C 5-CD album

Living in the Balance of Grace and Faith

This book explains one of the biggest controversies in the church today. Is it grace or faith that releases the power of God? Does God save people in His sovereignty, or does your faith move Him? You may be surprised by the answers as Andrew reveals what the Bible has to say concerning these important questions and more. This understanding will help you receive from God in a greater way and will change the way you relate to Him.

Item Code: 301B Paperback

The Believer's Authority

Like it or not, every one of us is in a spiritual war. You can't be discharged from service, and ignorance of the battlefield only aids the enemy. In war, God is always for us, and the devil is against us; whichever one we cooperate with will win. And there's only one way the enemy can get your cooperation—that's through deception. In this teaching, Andrew exposes this war and the enemy for what he is.

Item Code: 1045-C	6-CD album
Item Code: 1045-D	DVD album (as recorded from television)

The Effects of Praise

Every Christian wants a stronger walk with the Lord. But how do you get there? Many don't know the true power of praise. It's essential. Listen as Andrew teaches biblical truths that will spark not only understanding but will help promote spiritual growth so you will experience victory.

Item Code: 309	Paperback
Item Code: 1004-C	3-CD album

God Wants You Well

Health is something everyone wants. Billions of dollars are spent each year trying to retain or restore health. So why does religion tell us that God uses sickness to teach us something? It even tries to make us believe that sickness is a blessing. That's just not true. God wants you well!

Item Code: 1036-C	4-CD album